STOPPING EMPLOYEE THEFT

WHAT EVERY EMPLOYER MUST KNOW

R.W. DECKERT

Diverse Assets Creations, Inc., Publisher

ISBN: 0-9662640-0-2

Library of Congress Catalog Card Number:
98-92501

Typesetting by Maryland Composition

Printing by United Book Press, Inc.

Printed in USA.

Diverse Assets Creations, Inc
Box 2265, Columbia, MD. 21045
Interstate# 888-403-3325
Fax# 410-792-0468

Acknowledgments

There are many people to thank for making this book possible. I must start from the beginning, with those insurance claims specialists that have supported me with insurance losses for many years. Without Patty Duffy, CPCU., Sheri Moser O'Donoghue, Don Thompson, AIC., John O'Donoghue, Claims Manager, Royal Insurance Company, Mary Mason, Burleigh Turner, Claims Manager, Royal Insurance Company and Sherry Beahm, Regional Claims Manager, Montgomery Mutual Insurance Company, I doubt I would have acquired the expertise I now have in this subject. Many thanks for your confidence in me.

Several professionals offered their assistance in subjects discussed in many chapters. Without their input some topics would not be as helpful to the reader.

I hope I can someday return the favor to:

Jim Kern, CPA
Gross Mendelsohn & Assoc.
Certified Public Accountants

*

Dave Gilliss, Esquire
Niles, Barton and Wilmer
Attorneys at Law

*

Michael Loughran
Director of Human Resources
Kennedy Krieger Institute

*

Jack McGovern
Claims Specialist
Royal Insurance Co.
Charlotte, NC.

Special thanks go to two professionals for their review and editing of specific sections of text:

Evelyn S. Brunner, CPA,
Schiller, Holinsky and Gardyn, PA.
Certified Public Accountants

*

W. Wm. Cookson, CPCU.

Words fall short in trying to thank my two main editors, Matt Gutberlet and Jan Deckert. Without their input, and grammatical assistance I do not think the content would read as well as it does.

Finally, thanks to my family; my wife Jan, daughters Holly and Lauren and my mother, for patience, encouragement, sacrifice and support that began in January of 1997, when I started transferring notes from paper to computer.

R. W. Deckert

TABLE OF CONTENTS

Chapter Five

Chapter Six

Chapter Seven

Subrogation, Recovery
Restitution **77**

INTRODUCTION

The purpose of this book is to save your hard-earned money and possibly your entire life's work from the real prospects of theft from within your business, professional practice or corporation.

In writing this book, I have provided detailed information and case histories on all aspects of employee theft. This information should provide a better understanding for employers, risk managers, accountants, attorneys and insurance professionals on this important and complicated subject. The scope of the book will encompass the following:

- The material will detail the who and the what that is covered under the majority of policies issued to cover employers for theft by their employees.
- The reader will learn **what to do** should theft be discovered, and how best to work with the thief and your other employees.
- The text will cover the **adjustment** or claim process, **police involvement, subrogation** and **recovery procedures**, as well as **who** is a thief and **why** he steals.
- The final chapters will explore the various **methods of theft** used by many embezzlers, with **actual case summaries**, and the **management controls** that can minimize or prevent the chances of employee theft, if implemented and used from the time of hire.

Employee theft is a problem for every type of employer, from the large corporation to the small mom and pop run store. Depending on what source is quoted, the yearly loss to employers from employee theft is between 10 to 40 billion dollars a year. Most experts predict that one out of three employees will steal from their employer if given the opportunity.

For over twenty years in my insurance career, I have investigated employee theft losses in professional practices, businesses and industries. My experience has been as an independent adjuster or investigator retained primarily by insurance or bonding companies to investigate all aspects of a claim for employee theft. This subject used to be referred to as "Fidelity Bonds," then later known as "Employee Theft," and now as "Employee Dishonesty", but it is all the same thing, money out of the employer's company, and into the hands of an embezzler.

During these years of investigation I was left with the feeling that many employers did not have all the information that they needed in order to properly protect themselves prior to and after a theft or loss occurred. I felt that the insurance industry did more towards promoting loss control and insured's education in fire and worker's compensation losses than in the area of employee theft. It has only been in the last few years that I have noticed some insurance industry professionals taking a more active approach to the employee theft exposure. (Still, based on my experiences, there are many insurance agents, accountants, and their clients, the employers, that need guidance in this area.) I felt this book would answer a lot of questions, and for the first time provide a comprehensive guide to this difficult exposure.

Since different insurers **Bonded** a broad spectrum of insureds and companies, it allowed me to be exposed to a significant number of methods that employees used to steal from their employers. During the course of this book you will learn many of the methods that were used. This is necessary so one can achieve a better understanding of what was done, and by taking and using this information, minimize the chances of theft in their own company. Some may think that by providing information on methods of theft, that I am supplying education for those who may use it against an employer. Granted this information has value to all who read it, but the employer has the advantage of being able to place into effect what I call **Management Controls.** These controls, if followed as I outline in this work, will make it very difficult for an employee to sustain any type of significant theft from his or her employer.

Where I refer to an actual case I will use the word **CASE HISTORY** before going into the facts of the case. Some discussion on how a theft was done will follow, but in the chapters dealing with

METHODS OF THEFT AND MANAGEMENT CONTROLS, detailed explanations will be given in many cases. Unless otherwise noted, I personally conducted all the investigations that are covered in the "case histories".

You will note that there are no employer or company names used in any cases that I refer to. There are several reasons for that.

- Some employers did not pursue their losses through the police and criminal courts because they did not want the general public, or in some cases competitors or corporate benefactors, to know about their experiences.
- Some cases are new and still in the litigation stages and it would be improper to mention names.

I have used employees first names in some histories, just to break from the use of the word "employee", "thief", "embezzler", etc. I also interchange use of the pronouns **he and she** only to change from using the same word repeatedly. The use of one pronoun over the other is not an indication that a certain gender is more or less likely to steal as a result of a specific employment position.

You will also see that I do not mention individual insurance company names when discussing the various employee dishonesty policies, or the bonding companies that I conducted investigations for. I do not wish to show favoritism to any company that writes this type of business. This book should encourage employers to work closer with their insurance agents in designing a plan of coverage that best suits that employer. There are many insurance companies that can quote on this type of risk. In mentioning six or seven companies, by name, would be unfair to others that I may not be as familiar with, but who may have as good or better plan for an employer than the ones whose names I use. The employer's insurance agent is best qualified to comment on individual insurance carriers.

Because I wanted this book to be as helpful as possible, it will acquaint you with the definitions of some of the insurance and legal terminology before reading the text. This will enable you to have a better understanding of the book's content. Therefore, the first chapter will explain many key words used in this study.

Finally you will note that this book is brief in length due to the fact that I feel anyone that runs a business, professional practice or corporation does not have time to read voluminous text on this subject. All you as the employer really want to know is:

- How much employee dishonesty coverage should I have

- What kind of coverage do I need for my business

- How do I prevent employee theft

- How do I recognize a problem involving employee theft

- If I do have a theft, how do I deal with it

Chapter One

Insurance and Legal Terms

You, Employer, Insured- These words are interchangeable throughout this book.

Insurance or Bonding Company- The words insurance and bonding are interchangeable. They refer to a state licensed insurance company that underwrites the risk for employee theft. The policy and the amount of coverage can be for a specific position such as Financial Officer, or can be written in blanket form where there is a specific amount of coverage for all employees, or one employee working alone or in collusion with others.

When using the word "bond policy" in this study it will always refer to "employee theft," not other types of bonds.

Insurance Agent-refers to the individual licensed insurance professional that completes the application for the coverage with you. This is the person that you should contact when you need to report a loss under the policy.

Insurance Adjuster/Investigator-this is either an employee of an insurance company or an independent contractor that is retained on a per case basis to investigate all or part of an employee theft loss.

Public Adjuster-this is a state licensed insurance professional hired by the insured to represent them during all aspects of the loss and claim. The PA, as they are referred to, enters into a written contract with insured and normally charges a percentage of the paid loss as his fee for his services. This percentage will vary depending on what the insured wants the PA to do and the amount of the loss. A 6 to 10% amount is average.

Even though the PA is the link between the insured and the adjuster/investigator, the policy still requires that the insured cooperate with the insurance company or its representative. This could mean meetings, statements, and interviews with other employees.

Private Investigator-a state licensed individual, usually a former police, military or federal law enforcement officer. A "PI" can enter into a contract with the employer to investigate all aspects of the loss on behalf of the employer. He or she can also be used to conduct background checks on proposed employees or any other legal investigation or surveillance that the employer wants done. The expense incurred for the PI's services are not covered under any policy, so they must be paid by the employer.

Fidelity Proof of Loss-An insurance document that summarizes the information about the theft, who the employer believes is responsible, when the loss was discovered and the amount of that loss. Unlike other proof of losses, the fidelity proof is completed before the insurance company conducts its investigation, outside of contact with the employer. This provides the insurance company with protection in that it is not the insurance company making the allegations of theft, it is the employer.

Shrinkage- Refers to an unexplained loss (decrease) of inventory from the insured. Historically shrinkage is thought to be caused by customer theft.

Manifest intent-Refers to the requirement that in order for an act or loss by employee theft to be covered under a standard employee dishonesty policy, the employee causing or responsible for the theft must "intend" or have purpose to (1) cause the employer to sustain a loss and (2) intend to provide financial benefit to the employee (himself) or another person. Both (1) and (2) are needed in order to have coverage. Additionally, the word "manifest" refers to: readily perceived, or obvious.

Bill of lading- Refers to a shipping document that list what was being shipped, the quantity shipped, by whom, and to what location.

Profit and loss computation- A vague, undefined term found in the bond policies that refers to any document, that is supposed to show whether the insured has suffered a loss of income, over a period of time, which the insured believes was as the result of employee theft.

Independent Contractor-someone who works for you but also works for other employers as well. An office or accounting temporary is an example of this. You do not take any taxes from the pay of the contractor. The contractor is paid a 1099 for any services rendered. Always check with your CPA before hiring someone that you want to place as an independent contractor, because the IRS laws can change concerning what qualifies as an independent contractor.

Subrogation-The process that the insurance company undertakes to try and recover for payments made under the policy or bond to the employer. The insurance company, not the employer has the legal right to recover that amount from the person or company responsible. Any amount that is not paid by the insurance company including any deductible, can still be paid directly to the employer.

Promissory note-This is what is signed by the employee after the amount of theft is agreed to. It calls for payments to be paid to the insurance company on a monthly bases. Interest is charged on the amount of loss. These notes are used when you have cooperation with the employee and there is no need to go to court.

Restitution-This term refers to the payments paid back to either the employer or the bonding company for the amount that was stolen. Usually the courts are involved, and will decide the amount to be paid per month. The court will sometimes garnish wages of the employee. Payments are made to the state and the state in turn pays either the employer or the insurance company.

Civil court-Where a legal action for the theft is brought either by the employer or the insurance company. If the court finds that the evidence supports the plaintiff (the employer or the insurance company) it will require restitution be made by the defendant (employee). The court can agree to allow attachment of property owned by the defendant and/or garnishment of wages.

Criminal court-Where legal action is brought by the state on behalf of the employer, not the insurance company. If the court finds the defendant guilty of embezzlement, the penalty can be incarceration, probation, or probation tied to restitution. This means that if the defendant fails to make timely payments to the state on behalf of the victims, the state can impose a prison sentence.

Chapter Two

What is Employee Theft

For the most part employee theft involves the stealing or embezzling of money or inventory from the employer, by a currently employed or recently terminated individual, or groups of persons working in a conspiracy, for the purpose of their financial gain at the loss of the employer. Under one of the most frequently written policy forms, CR 00 01, it reads: **"Employee Dishonesty"in paragraph A.2. means only dishonest acts committed by an "employee" whether identified or not, acting alone or in collusion with other persons, except you or a partner, with the manifest intent to:**

1. **Cause you to sustain loss; and also**
2. **Obtain financial benefit (other than employee benefits earned in the normal course of employment, including; salaries, commissions, fees, bonuses, promotions, awards, profit sharing or pensions) for:**

   (a) **The "employee"; or**
   (b) **Any person or organization intended by the "employee" to receive that benefit.**

An explanation of some of these words are in order:

"Dishonest acts" refer to some sort of stealing, embezzlement or forgery, type activity.

"Employee" means an actual person that you pay a salary or commission to. It can also mean someone you terminated up to 30 days before an employee theft is discovered. (There are many other important points in this definition, and they are discussed in chapter 3.)

"Identified or not" refers to whether you know who the employee is that has stolen from you. (This is discussed further in chapter 3).

"Acting alone or in collusion with others" refers to the insurance company accepting, under one deductible and listed as one loss, all the losses or damages caused by an employee or several employees working together, even though there may be several different actual thefts. Non-employees working with an "employee" do not jeopardize the coverage.

"Except you or a partner" refers to an exclusion that does not allow payment of an employee theft loss if one of the persons involved is the owner of the business or a partner.

"Manifest intent" is one of the requirements for coverage. The words "manifest intent" have been subjected to several interpretations by claims people, insurance companies and the courts. You should consult with your own insurance agent or insurance attorney for **their** interpretation of the wording.

My interpretation is that "manifest intent" should be considered in all losses between the employee and the employer as well as in third party cases. I feel it requires that the employee know, without any doubt, that his employer is going to suffer a loss as a result of the employee's actions, and that either the employee or someone that the employee selects will receive a financial benefit from that theft.

CASE HISTORY: The manager for an auto dealer confessed that he stole nearly $30,000 because his adult son was a drug addict, had no money, and needed it for drug rehabilitation costs.

CASE HISTORY: A large janitorial contractor received a call that one of their employees was caught by the police stealing stereo components from the client's store. Investigation by the police confirmed that there had been other thefts and the stolen com-

ponents sold on the street. The employee confessed to several thefts over a three month period.

In order for the client to recover from the insurance company of the employer, there were a number of requirements.

- *There had to be employee dishonesty coverage in place for the employee that stole the merchandise.*
- *The employee must not have been discovered stealing prior to this particular theft.*
- *The employer had to be convinced that this was employee theft, verify the damages and make a payment to the client. (As you will read in the coverage chapter, this is coverage for benefit of the employer, and all payments are made to the employer).*

If the bonding company agreed with the loss amount, and there were no other coverage violations, the employer had to pay the client and the bonding company would then consider payment to the employer.

In the above case a payment was made by the bonding company of the janitorial service. The insurance company paid their insured after receiving copies of payments that the insured made to their client. In reviewing this case nine years later, my recommendation now, would have been that the "manifest intent"wording would probably have kept the insurance company from having to make any payment. It is difficult to visualize the employee thinking that his employer is going to sustain a loss because the employee is stealing from a client of the employer. (The loss was paid because of the "legal liability clause in the policy). This will be discussed in Chapter 4.

"Manifest intent" or lack of it comes into consideration when an unhappy employee "sabotages" the employer's equipment or property, because the employee did not get the raise she felt she deserved. There was no intent to receive financial benefit herself, only cause a loss for the employer.

Additionally, if an employee steals money from the employer and burns it in a fireplace, the employer has sustained a loss, but the employee did not receive financial benefit in the meaning of the policy. (This benefit is not required in new "combined crime forms" that I will discuss in chapter 4).

"Cause you to sustain loss" means that the employer has to suffer actual damages, is also one of the requirements for coverage. These damages or "loss" can be money, securities, or stock, inventory or equipment. It can also mean that you, the employer sustains a loss if you must pay someone else for their damages or loss due to the "employee theft" of your employee.

"Obtain financial benefit (other than employee benefits earned in the normal course of employment)," etc., is another requirement for coverage and along with "manifest intent" has caused the most debate concerning whether a loss is covered or not. The controversy usually centers around the question of "salary " and "commissions". Courts have ruled that if an employee uses fraudulent methods to increase his or her salary, that loss is not covered under the bond because it is just additional salary. An example is a manager that submits false orders of new business, in turn she is paid salary and commissions based on that "new business". Eventually the scheme is discovered, and the employer files a employee theft loss. However, the insurance company does not make a voluntary payment because it was salary that was involved.

CASE HISTORY: *An auto dealer was contacted by a bank that financed many of the cars sold by the dealership. The bank manager found that there were many more repossessions coming from this dealership as compared to other dealerships in the area. The insured investigated and found that his Finance and Insurance Manager was putting through a number of people with very questionable credit, or placing them in cars that were above what it appeared the people could afford. Since the F and I manager received a commission on the number of deals he put through, the insured felt this was employee theft.*

The investigation found that there was a sales manager in the dealership, over the F and I manager, that had a right to reject any deal. Furthermore, the bank had the final say on any loan. Since neither individual above the F nd I manager rejected the applications, it was not felt that the additional commissions paid to the manager or the losses that the bank took when they had to sell the vehicles at auction were recoverable under the bond.

The above example and the "case history" must be compared to a situation where the employee benefits by stealing checks, paying herself additional monies by forging the owners signature, negotiating the checks and keeping the money. None of this money is recorded as salary, there are no taxes taken out. It is an obvious attempt to embezzle money from the employer. (You will read about several of these schemes in chapter 10). In my opinion, and that of the insurance companies involved in these cases, these were not examples of the "benefits earned in the normal course of employment..." that **was** evident in the example where coverage was denied.

One word that seems to describe employee theft losses is the word **"insidious."** The dictionary defines insidious as "sly,treacherous, having a gradual and cumulative effect". These words fit this type of theft like a glove. In many cases the employer will not have any idea that the theft has been going on, sometimes for years at a time.

Usually the thief will begin with small amounts taken over relatively long periods of time. As the thief realizes that no one has caught on to his activity, he increases the amounts taken, and also the frequency of the thefts. Eventually due to employee error or the amount of money or stock making a significant dent in the operation of the company, an investigation is begun and usually the employee is caught.

CASE HISTORY: *There was a large auto dealer that hired an experienced car man to run the new car prep operation. Part of the manager's job was to order the undercoating that was used to spray on the chassis' of new cars before delivery. This employee started a company that would bill the auto dealer (employer) for the undercoating. The employee typed his own invoice, sent it to* *his (the new car prep manager) attention at the dealership, where he wrote "approved" on the invoice, and sent it to accounting for payment. When I became involved I noticed the initial "sales" were small and infrequent. Eventually they became larger and larger.*

Auto and truck dealerships keep volumes of records on expenses and profits on all departments. These printouts give the dealer a comparison of each department to similar departments in other dealerships. The greed was so flagrant that the amount of expense in the new car department was so far above the sister dealerships that the owner began an investigation. By checking the invoices of undercoating he had purchased, the dealer discovered two things. First that he paid for enough undercoating to service new cars for several years, and that the address of the vending "company" was the home address of his manager. The owner of the dealership told me that had the employee not increased the purchases to the extent that he had, the theft could have gone on for a long period of time.

One must separate embezzlement from poor business practice even though the employer may lose in either case. If an employee makes poor business decisions that cost the company money or loss of stock (inventory), that does not qualify as theft under the bond policy. The key is whether the employee's actions result in the employee making a financial gain over and above his or her normal source of income from that employer.

CASE HISTORY: There was a sales company that gave their sales representatives expense accounts. Included on that expense account was the allowance of taking clients to lunch and dinners as well as buying the clients gifts for their business. After an audit of one sales rep's. account the employer questioned some rather expensive gifts and four star type entertainment. The employer wanted to file a claim under the bond for these expenses, but the actions were not done with the intent of the employee to make a financial gain, so no payment was made.

Another situation that presents itself occasionally concerns **inventory shortage.** This term refers to a claim of loss of inventory (stock) or an unexplained loss of money (profits). If it is a loss of inventory, the discovery of a possible loss normally surfaces when a year end audit or inventory of stock, product etc. is completed and found to be short. "Short" refers to the fact that the actual inventory is less than what purchase invoices and sales records show should be on hand. If it is a loss of money, that could be discovered during a weekly total of sales figures or from an accountant's audit representing a longer time period. Sometimes the term used by the insured is that the "cost of goods" has increased with no other explanation for the increase, therefore it must be from employee theft.

Losses that come under the heading of "inventory shortage", are excluded under the bond coverage. It is not the intent or purpose of the bond to consider loss that may be due to poor inventory control, losses from customer theft or inaccurate record keeping of purchases and sales.

In order for the employer to receive consideration in these circumstances, they must show that employee theft has taken place. It should be noted that if the employer is able to prove to the satisfaction of the insurance company that an employee theft has taken place, and if the employee theft can be tied to the inventory shortage, then it is possible to use the inventory shortage record as a measure of the extent of the embezzlement.

I use the word possible, because the facts of every case are different and the amount of weight to place on what the employee stole in relation to what is claimed to have been stolen can be viewed and accepted differently by each bonding company.

I will discuss two cases so you will have a better idea of inventory shortage.

CASE HISTORY: *There was a small steel fabricating company that discovered an office clerk had stolen money from the office. She would work late at night supposedly to catch up on paper work, but what she was doing was waiting for every one to leave before she began her theft. The company's accounts payable checks were generated from a continuous feed computer check* stock. In other words the checks were on one long sheet of computer paper. In most of these continuous runs, the first one or two checks are blank because the printer has not caught up with the computer command. Carol would take these checks and type her name in as the payee. She would then find the signature stamp of the employer and "sign his name". She would negotiate the check at her bank. Carol also did the bank statements, so she was able to prolong the theft. However, her scheme was eventually discovered. During the adjustment process the employer tried to include some "unexplained inventory loss" as part of Carol's theft. In my investigation, Carol admitted to the theft from the office and all check numbers used by her were found. As far as we could tell she had no contacts with anyone in the shipping or receiving areas, where the loss of inventory was coming from. We could not find any conspiracy. The employer never presented any bogus invoices similar to the car dealer situation, and could not provide any other documents or investigation to show that there was an employee behind his loss or shortage of inventory. All he had was an increase in expenses and a decrease in profits, but no other documents to support the loss.

    The end result was yes, there was a theft by an employee, and yes, there was a payment made for the check scheme, but no payment was made for the inventory loss.

Compare those facts with this one.

CASE HISTORY: There was a retail business that sold car stereos, CDs, and other small stereo components. The owner received a telephone call from someone who said that he bought a car stereo from an installer that worked in that section of the store. Apparently, the buyer knew that the stereo was stolen and had second thoughts about the purchase.

    The employer obtained the stereo piece from the buyer and after determining that this particular item, based on its serial number should still be on the shelf, interviewed the employee. The owner determined that a theft had taken place and filed an employee theft loss.

During the employer's checking of the status of their stock, many inventory items were found to be missing. Prior to the phone call from the customer, the employer had no idea that employee theft had been going on. All of the other missing inventory items were of the type that this particular employee had access to. Even though the employee denied taking all of the inventory claimed, the employer was able to use that one verified stolen item to increase the amount of covered loss.

When I use the words "currently employed" I am referring to the requirement that there be an employee/employer relationship at the time the thefts took place, not that the employee still be employed when the thefts are discovered. Usually the existence of theft will be discovered while the person responsible is still employed, but not always. The key to insurance coverage is the date of the theft in relation to when the person was employed. Sometimes the difference can be only a matter of days but can mean the difference between coverage and no payment.

CASE HISTORY: There was a company that built cabinets for a specific medical field professional group. The company had master drawings for these cabinets. Unfortunately, they did not have a second set. One of their employees, also one of the craftsmen, quit because he did not get the raise in pay he felt he deserved. Several days after the termination, the office was broken into and the drawings stolen. The company had heard that this particular, now ex employee, had said he wanted to start his own company. The police were contacted and the ex-employee admitted that he took the drawings. He also said he did not have them anymore.

*The employee theft policy that this insured had was a form that did not have coverage for theft by an employee, up to thirty days after termination. The policy wording on this form did not mention any coverage after termination. The interpretation was that the employee **must** be employed at the time of the theft.*

Since the police report confirmed the break-in date was after the employee quit, there was no coverage under the bond.

You may think to yourself that all the employer needed to do was file a claim for theft under a crime policy; however, they did not have that coverage. This will be discussed in more detail in the coverage chapter.

Earlier I wrote that quite often the thief is still employed when the loss is **discovered**. That is not always the case however, and although it does not occur often, there have been cases where the employee was no longer employed when the loss was discovered.

This type of loss discovery usually takes place from an audit, or investigation begun when the annual report shows that profits are not what they should be, or when vendors or clients call looking for payment that is long overdue. (Frankly, I am surprised that more embezzlers don't leave before they are discovered. Most methods of theft cannot go on forever and are discovered eventually). Comments about why they may not leave before they are found out will be discussed in Chapter 8..

The important point here is that there **can be** coverage for theft that took place during the time of employment, but not discovered until after termination or separation of the employee, as long the losses took place during the policy period and were discovered no more then one year after the end of the policy period. (The amount of time allowed differs in some policies). This will be covered in Chapter 4.

CASE HISTORY: A stereo retailer had a customer bring in a unit for servicing. When the serial number was checked, it was determined that the unit had been brought in several months earlier for repair, by a different customer. Inventory records showed that the item was still in the repair inventory. Through additional questions the customer admitted that he bought the unit from someone that used to work at the store.

This employee, Ted, worked in the repair department and did have access to the room where the units were stored. Ted had left the company two months earlier. After the police investigated, the ex-employee admitted to the theft. The loss occurred during the employment period and was covered even though the employee was not employed when the loss was discovered.

This chapter has provided the basis for what employee theft is. The next chapter will discuss who is an employee, and who is covered, and when coverage stops.

Chapter Three

Who is an Employee, Who is Covered

This coverage is for the benefit of the employer that sustains a covered loss by one or more employees working alone or in conspiracy with others. The **"others"** can be employees or non- employees. The CR 00 01 form seems to be the one that is used more often in employee dishonesty coverage. For that reason I am going to use that form for the topic in this chapter.

Under the standard Employee Dishonesty Coverage Form:(CR 00 01) **Employee Dishonesty means only dishonest acts committed by an "employee", whether identified or not, acting alone or in collusion with other persons, except you or a partner . . .**

The word **"Employee"** in this form means:

  a. **Any natural person:**

    1. **While in your service (and 30 days after service), and**
    2. **Whom you compensate directly by salary, wages or commissions, and**
    3. **Whom you have the right to direct and control while performing services for you, or**

  b. **Any natural person employed by an employment contractor while performing services for you, excluding however, any such person while having care and custody of property outside the "premises."**

The wording **"identified or not"** requires an explanation. In older bond forms the employer had to name the individual that had stolen from him. If a loss had taken place, but the employer was not sure which employee was responsible, he could not legally name a specific employee on the fidelity proof of loss form.

CASE HISTORY: The insured operated a pizza parlor. He would normally have one manager and several employees working any one shift. The sales from each shift were totaled by the manager and placed in the safe located in a small office in the back of the store. On one particular shift the manager forgot to put the money and deposit slip in the safe; instead it was left on the desk. The manager returned to the front of the store to assist his crew. The office door did not lock automatically when the door was shut. When the manager returned he noticed that the money was missing.

There were four employees that worked that shift. All could have found time to enter the office and remove the deposit and money. Plus, the office was in the hall that led to the bathrooms, so customers would also walk by the office door and could possibly have gone into the office. (I felt that scenario was doubtful; it seemed unlikely that a customer would be bold enough to open a solid metal door and walk into an office.)

By placing a specific employee name on the proof of loss form, the employer is stating that that employee stole from him. If the employer were wrong, the employee could have a legal action for libel against the employer.

Because the employer would not name a specific employee, the claim was denied and no payment made. Under the newer forms (except the CR 00 02) the employer can write in the word "unidentified" where it requests the name of the employee involved. This is much better coverage for the insured. There are going to be situations where there is no question that employee theft has taken place, but the employer may not discover, even after an investigation, which employee was responsible.

Please remember that the definition or meaning of the word employee as it relates to coverage under a bond policy can differ depending on the policy form used. It is imperative that the employer know which form is being written by his insurance agent and how that form relates to the employer's hiring practices.

CLASSIFICATION OF EMPLOYEES:

Over the lifetime of a company or professional practice there will be several classifications of employees that will work within the company. Some of these are covered under the bond, others excluded.The first class of employees are the **officers of the company.** Under current IRS laws an officer of the corporation can still be an employee and as such can be covered under most employee theft coverage.

An officer of a company can be an employee as well as a stock holder\partner\co owner. If he or she is a partner then coverage under the bond is usually not extended to that person.

The wording of **"except you or a partner"** in the above definition makes that point quite clear. It is not the intent of the bond policy to insure the illegal actions or theft by the owner himself from himself. However, in cases where a minority **stockholder not a partner** stole money from the majority stockholder, it would seem unfair for the corporation to suffer the loss because a 10% stock holder, also an employee, embezzled funds from the company. As I wrote above, a stock holder can still be an employee, and as such is covered under the bond form.

Another situation that is not common, should also be included in this section in case a reader finds him or herself in this predicament. This occurs when you have an individual who is a stockholder and officer, receiving profits from the corporation as his only income from the company but still **functions as an employee does**.

CASE HISTORY: There was a corporation that operated bar\arcade type establishments in several cities. Barry was the manager of one of the stores, he was also minority stock holder, past president of the company, and a current vice president and director. Part of his duties was to make up the daily deposit and take it to the bank. He stole the deposits. (I discuss this case at length in Chapter 11, so I will not repeat the details here).

The point I want to make is that after our investigation, it was the position of the bonding company that Barry was not an employee under the above definition. He did not receive compensation as defined in the policy form. It states, "salary, wages or commissions." He received none of these, only a payment at the end of the fiscal year from profits of the corporation.

It was also the position of the bonding company that he was an owner and director and since he was in essence stealing from himself the company would not pay the loss.

It was my recommendation not to pay the claim, but I made a comment about a specific passage in the coverage that could cause a court to rule in favor of the employer. Referring to the CRIME GENERAL PROVISIONS (CR 10 00), under GENERAL DEFINITIONS; after b. (found on the first page of this chapter) the following words: **But "employee" does not mean any:**

(1) Agent, broker, factor, commission merchant, consignee, independent contractor or representative of the same general character;

(2) Director or trustee **except while performing acts coming within the scope of the usual duties of an employee.**

Therefore, you had a situation where Barry was not an employee by definition since he was not paid as an employee. He was an owner and trustee which further excluded him from coverage, but as manager he was to total the deposits and take them to the bank. This was an employee function that other managers did at other locations. Because of this wording I was told that the company settled the loss with the insured on a compromise basis.

As to other employee classifications, the bond policies are both liberal and strict when it comes to coverage requirements and allowances. These conditions refer primarily to the type policy where there is one single amount listed for all employees. For example, the bond policies do not make any distinction between full or part time employees, nor is there any waiting period before coverage takes effect. An employee hired the day before he stole would be covered, assuming other policy conditions had not been violated. The wording in these bond forms favors the insured when there is a theft that takes place over a period of time, but involving the same employee.

Under any other crime policy, each date that a theft occurs qualifies as a new loss. Thus any deductible would apply each time. In reality it is very rare that an insured suffers two or more losses of the same type, such as burglary or non-employee theft one after the other. These do occur from time to time. I have had a number of construction tools and equipment stolen from the same job sites, as well as the same hospital making claims for loss of expensive surgical and diagnostic equipment stored in poorly secured equipment rooms. Thefts from warehouses or stockrooms are another source of thefts that can involve more than one date of loss. There would be a deductible applied for each date, even if the thefts were being done by the same person, group or gang.

In employee theft it is unusual for there to be only one isolated theft. As I stated in my introduction, the thief steals in small amounts at first, and with dates of those thefts separated by days or weeks, sometimes several weeks. After gaining confidence, the amounts taken and frequency of those thefts increase.

Under the bond wording **"Occurrence"** means all loss caused by, or involving, one or more "employees"whether the result of a single act or series of acts. To have each theft be a separate incident with a deductible for each would be unfair to the insured. There is a very good reason for that. I have had cases where the number of thefts done by the same employee to the same employer totaled over 100.

CASE HISTORY: *There was a truck stop restaurant manager named Kathy. Her employer's main office was located in another state. Kathy normally worked the 12 to 8 AM shift. All restaurant sales were computerized. Kathy was able to change the computer so it did not record the sales from the night shift, and pocket the amount of that shift. (This case is discussed in detail in chapter 11).*

The point here concerns number of losses. When I became involved and requested all the backup documentation, it filled over eight boxes each at least 18 inches long and a foot wide. If each occurrence was a separate deductible of $250, the insured's $75,000 loss would have been reduced by $25,000.

Another classification of **"employee"** is perhaps the most difficult one for me to understand being placed under the same bond as regular employees. I am referring to **"temporary help"** those men and women that are paid hourly by temporary agencies. They come into your office to work anywhere from one day to several months. You have no idea who this person is, or what their background might be.Yet, under definition of Employee b. found in the General Crime Provisions they come under your employee theft coverage. The definition states: any natural person employed by an employment contractor "while that person is under your direction and control and performing services for you excluding, however, any such person while having care and custody of property outside the "premises".

This coverage is very liberal because it protects your company from someone you know very little about. It is in direct contradiction to what I am covering in this book. You will learn in a subsequent chapter titled **"Management Controls"** what a smart employer must do to minimize the chance of employee dishonesty or theft involving these "office temps."

Granted, it is to your benefit from a loss standpoint that should this "temp" steal from you, that you would have coverage. But what happens to morale in your company if the theft causes cash flow problems, or if the loss exceeds your coverage, or if he or she involves a client of yours and you lose that client's future business.

CASE HISTORY: There was a case involving an office placement company that was the insured of the bonding company. The client of the insured had need of office help due to illness in his staff, and he contacted the insured for a "temp." Janice came to work around Christmas time and worked Christmas Eve after everyone else went home. Janice had quickly learned where the owner of the company kept company checks. She took several checks, forged the owner's signature, made herself the payee and was able to negotiate them at the bank. In only a few days *she had stolen over $12,000. She left her "temp job" as well as the placement agency before the checks came back through the bank statement.*

This loss caused several problems for the client, one of which was an overdrawn business account because funds in the account were not sufficient to cover the checks. Janice took the checks from the back of the check book so the missing checks were not noticed.

The client relied on the placement service to send over a qualified and honest employee. There wasn't time, nor did the client **think or know** what to do to minimize the chance of employee theft by this person.

During the course of the investigation I explained to the client that **his** employee theft coverage would cover him for the loss. The president of the company was not happy about that. The owner wanted to file a claim under the placement agency coverage. I do not think he was going to use the placement service again. You will read in chapter 4 where I discuss the newer combined crime forms that state the insured's bond coverage is "excess" or "secondary" over any primary coverage written through the temporary agency's coverage. I predict that all bond coverage will have this wording eventually. In my meeting with the insured I found out that the manager did have Janice complete an application for employment but there was no question of past criminal history. When the insured provided Janice's full name, I recognized it from a bond loss I had five years earlier. Janice worked for a Health Provider and embezzled $35,000 in several months from them. She was caught, did several years in jail, came out and went right back to her "profession".

Remember, any time a loss occurs you will have to give up some of your time to assist in the investigation of the loss. This can include statements to investigators, gathering your loss documentation, police interviews, and court appearances. All this time takes away from running your business, company or practice. And, that time lost, is not recoverable under the bond policy.

Finally the loss will go against your loss experience with the insurance company. That could have an effect on your future insurance coverage and premium.

As you can see, if you use temporary help you have an exposure that can be very costly. However, there are procedures to follow to minimize this exposure, and this will be covered in "management controls."

The final area of employee classification is **independent contractors**. The bond policy does not cover them. You should check with your accountant or CPA to make certain that the relationship you have with this individual qualifies for independent contractor status.

WHEN COVERAGE FOR AN EMPLOYEE STOPS:

There are two very important provisions of the CR 00 01 form that concern when coverage for a specific employee stops. The policy wording for the first provision is as follows: **We will not pay for loss as specified below:**

1. Employee cancelled under prior bond: loss caused by any "employee" of yours, or predecessor of interest of yours, for whom similar prior insurance has been cancelled and not reinstated since the last such "cancellation."

My interpretation of the above is that if there is an employee that works for you now, but who had committed a dishonest act while working for a company that you **now** own or control, and as a result of that dishonest act he or she was no longer covered under that bond, coverage cannot be extended to that employee under any new bond coverage.

The second similar provision reads as follows:

2. **Cancellation as to any employee: This insurance is cancelled to any "employee,"**

   a. Immediately upon discovery by:

      1. You; or
      2. Any of your partners, officers or directors not in collusion with the "employee" of any dishonest act committed by that "employee" whether before or after becoming employed by you.

This part means that as soon as one of the officers in the company finds out about any employee stealing, **any future thefts** by that employee are not covered by the bond. This exclusion also means that if an employee had stolen years before coming to work with you, and if you are aware of that history, any theft by that employee is not covered. I have had this occur quite often.

CASE HISTORY: There was a car dealer that had a very small office staff. One day the office deposit of nearly $3,000 was missing. After being unable to locate the money a bond claim was made. During the investigation one of the cashiers was discovered to have taken the money. However, in the statement taken from the employee, she admitted having taken a smaller amount in a previous theft. This had been reported to the owner who gave the cashier another chance. This information was confirmed with the insured. Based on this the company denied payment of the $3,000 loss.

Although it may be commendable that the employer wanted to give the young lady a second chance, the bond policy is not that benevolent. The employer should have either terminated the employee after the first loss was discovered, or at least put her in a position where it would be difficult for her to steal from him.

In Chapter nine **"Management Controls, Pre-Employment"** I write about the importance of having a thorough employment application. But a complete application is not any good if the employer does not read it or know the policy wording concerning previous dishonest actions. Here are case histories.

CASE HISTORY: One of my first employee theft investigations involved a night auditor employed by a large hotel chain. The auditor was able to steal over $15,000 before he was discovered. The management retained an out of state Public Adjuster to represent them. One of the first things that I requested in an investigation of this type was a complete copy of the employee's per-

sonal file. Any employment application would be a part of that file. In reviewing the application I noted that the employee had a conviction for felony theft, had spent time in jail and was on parole. Clearly this was a violation of the bond wording concerning previous dishonest acts. After submitting this information to the bonding company the loss was denied.

I should note here that I asked the managing partner if he was aware of the employee's history, he said that he was, but did not know that the policy wording would disallow any coverage for that employee.

CASE HISTORY: A large construction company was experiencing theft of power tools from a large job site. The first loss was treated as regular theft and paid by the insurance company under a contractor's equipment policy. When the second theft occurred, an employee of the company was discovered to have been involved. The insurance company retained me to investigate this second claim. The investigation by the police determined that the employee was responsible for both losses.

In reviewing the application of employment, the form asks if the applicant had any theft convictions. The employee answered that he did. Again this was a violation of the bond and the loss was denied by the carrier. I do not think the insurance company was able to recover from the insured what they paid on the first loss.

I asked the insured if he was aware of the employee's answer concerning past convictions, and he said that he had never been shown the application. I assume that a personnel officer decided to hire the individual and that person either did not read that part of the application or did not know of the policy wording. It is **very important that anyone on your staff that has any hiring authority become knowledgeable with the wording of the bond policy in place with your company.**

Additionally, your staff should be trained in reviewing key parts of the application as they pertain to what is this applicant's history besides education and previous job status. Whether you are a large corporation or a small operation, the exposure and requirements on your part are the same.

These last two chapters discussed definitions and examples of who and what is an employee. The next chapter will look into the major employee dishonesty policies, what is covered and how much coverage you should carry.

Chapter Four

Types of Coverage

What is Covered & How Much Coverage Should You Have

As stated previously, the intent of employee theft coverage or what is now referred to as **Employee Dishonesty Coverage** is to pay for loss or damage caused by an employee and sustained by the employer. Specific wording will depend on the policy selected by you and your insurance agent to cover your risk. It is very important that the agent be given a complete summary of your company situation so the appropriate coverage and dollar limit can be placed. To assist the agents in obtaining the information they need, there are **fidelity and crime questionnaires** that the agent will ask a company principal to complete.

There are several types of fidelity polices in the market place today. In this chapter, I will discuss two of the more frequently used policies seen in the investigations I have been involved with. I will also comment on other types of policies and some differences between them. This should give you a good idea of what is out there in the market of employee dishonesty coverage.

Two of the most common forms are the **Employee Dishonesty Coverage** under form: **CR 00 01**, and the **Business Owners Policy (BOP or BP2).** under form:**BP 00 02**, which allows Employee Dishonesty coverage as an option. This means that an extra premium must be paid to include that coverage.

The CR 00 01 form:) appears to be the most popular, and is written for small businesses up through large corporations. The BOP. policy as the name implies is written for a business, where the employee theft exposure is thought to be smaller. Normally the amount of coverage in the BOP policy is less than what I have found in the CR. policy. Every few years the forms are updated with current year dates but very little change in wording takes place. These policies are written with one limit of coverage, and that applies to all covered employees. This is called **blanket** coverage.

The limit in either policy is for any one occurrence, which means all covered losses from the action or actions of one employee or a group of employees, but acting together.

CASE HISTORY: Several years ago I investigated an employee theft loss involving an employee that was stealing inventory and equipment from the hospital where he worked. During the course of our investigation we discovered that a clerk in the office was stealing cash from that office. There was no indication that the two employees were working together, so the losses were two separate occurrences and as such two limits of coverage applied.

The CR. form is always issued with a **CRIME GENERAL PROVISIONS** form: **(CR 10 00)**. This CR 10 00 form explains the following areas of the policy; **General Exclusions, General Conditions, and General Definitions**. This form is used with any crime coverage bearing the CR policy designation. When I comment about any coverage wording in this form, I am referring to the CR. 00 01 and the CR 10 00 together.

The CR. form has more complete coverage than the BOP. endorsement, but the main coverages on both forms are similar:

- Both cover the loss of and loss from damage to property that results in a loss to the employer. The CR. form uses the wording "Covered Property" whereas the BOP. form uses the wording "Business Personal Property". You should check your individual policy for the definition of those two terms.

- The usual property involved is either **money**, which includes **cash** or **securities**, and also **inventory or stock**. Stock includes equipment used by the insured to operate whatever business they are in.
- Both forms require that the loss be by an employee with the manifest intent ... (see definition in first paragraph of Chapter two).

In order to have coverage, there must be a loss to the employer that falls within the covered property definition, and the employee must receive a benefit over the regular income and perks that were being received before the theft or dishonesty began. As to someone other than the employee receiving benefits it could be a relative.

CASE HISTORY: A Baltimore car dealer had sustained a substantial loss from an employee that had been with them for years. The loss was over $40,000. After the investigation was over and the employee had been caught, it was discovered that she had been stealing the money to pay for the medical bills of her very ill mother who had no medical coverage.

The CR. form allows coverage for employees of employment contractors working for you, but the BOP. form does not contain that wording.

Both forms will extend the discovery period up to one year from the end of the policy period. This means that if the policy ended on December 31, 1995, and the following December you discover an employee theft loss that took place during 1995, you would have coverage under these forms.

There is also the same coverage for **"loss sustained during prior insurance"** which states: **"if you, or any predecessor in interest, sustained loss during the period of any prior insurance that you or the predecessor in interest could have recovered under insurance except that the time within which to discover loss had expired, we will pay for it under this insurance, provided:**

(1) **The insurance became effective at the time of cancellation or termination of the prior insurance; and**
(2) **The loss would have been covered by this insurance had it been in effect when the acts or events causing the loss were committed or occurred.**

Here is an explanation of the above: you have coverage with ABC Insurance Company from July '93 to '94 and you then change companies to XYZ Insurance Company with effective dates of July '94 to '96. You discover in September '95 an employee theft loss with the initial dates of thefts going back to July 93. You can not file against the ABC Company because the policy states that the covered loss must be discovered no later than one year from the end of the policy period. But since you went directly from ABC to XYZ Company, XYZ will cover the loss if the policy with ABC would have covered the loss except for the discovery date limitation, and if there are no other violations that would exclude coverage under the XYZ policy.

A very important point for the employer or insured to know is that negligent action or improper management techniques or accounting procedures cannot bar recovery under any employee theft bond form. This means that even if the bonding company gave you suggestions on ways to control theft and you did not put them into action, the bonding company cannot deny coverage for your lack of management controls.

Additionally, an employee at one location is still an employee even if the loss occurs at a different location from where the employee works.

Furthermore, a part time or casual labor employee is covered. There is also no waiting period before coverage begins under these forms.

Both forms have exclusions that are similar. These include;

1. **Loss committed by you or a partner,**
2. **Proof of loss based only on inventory shortage or profit and loss computation,**
3. **Cancellation of any employee once the insured discovers a dishonest act by that employee. This goes back to the employee's previous employer.**

Some explanation of all three follows:

Concerning a loss "committed by a partner", that is not covered because your partner is considered an insured. It is against the principle of insurance to pay for a theft loss committed by the insured against himself.

Concerning the "profit and loss computation", as I wrote in the definition of terms (chapter 1), this is a vague word, not defined in the policies. The intent by the insurance industry is not to limit what is to be considered a profit and loss computation. If the industry wanted to narrow what was meant by the wording, they could have said "income statement" or "profit and loss statement." Because of the lack of definition, every case is decided on its own merits with the insurance company writing the risk deciding what they feel qualifies as a profit and loss computation. This leads to confusion and no real clear ruling by the industry.

For example, the daily totals of a liquor store or grocery store, are sometimes referred to as a "daily cash audit" or "weekly cash summary". They typically include all sales, charges, refunds and deposits made from sales. Are these to be considered "profit and loss computations". If the manager of the store totals the "daily cash audit" and discovers that his "cash on hand" is $2000 short, but they had no other indication of any theft, and cannot find any other error to account for the "shortage" does this qualify as a "loss based only on profit and loss computation". Some insurance, accounting or legal minds would feel that if there was no other indication of theft, that this "daily cash audit" would qualify as a "profit and loss computation" and would not cover the loss because of the "inventory loss" exclusion in the policy.

Others in the insurance industry might feel that this summary shows that the insured **had** a loss ($2,000) on a specific day, and that this "daily cash audit" **is** documentation of that loss. But, what if the insured **did** have a loss of this amount reflected by this document. How does the insurance company know that it is an "employee dishonesty loss"? Could a customer or vendor somehow have grabbed the money? Could one of the partners/owner of the company feel this is an easy way of collecting $2,000 tax free, plus receive reimbursement from the insurance carrier for the loss? It is because of these uncertainties that the bonding companies do not pay for "loss based only on inventory shortage or profit and loss computation".

Finally, the "cancellation of any employee" means that as soon as an officer, or director of the insured, or the insured himself, is made aware (discovers) of an employee's theft history, whether with the current employer or going back to the past employer, any **further loss by that employee is not covered.**

The CR. has considerable more wording than the BOP. Here are some of the more important points, found in the CR. that pertain to employee dishonesty. If there is a similar phrase in the BOP. I will comment. I have shortened some of the wording or made changes from the exact wording in the policy to help in the understanding of the phrase. For the most part, any additional wording from the BOP. policy will come from the main policy not the "Employee Dishonesty" optional coverage. However, unless there is specific wording in that optional section, the wording in the main policy would apply to all losses, even employee dishonesty.

Under **GENERAL EXCLUSIONS:**

Indirect loss: is not covered. This includes but is not limited to:

a. Your inability to realize income that you would have realized had there been no loss to the company because of this employee theft,

b. Payments of damages of any type for which you are legally liable, but the company will cover compensatory damages arising directly from a covered loss,

c. Payments or costs or fees or other expenses that you incur in establishing the existence or the amount of loss. (The BOP. policy pays only for"direct loss" as well; there are a number of exclusions and limitations but they do not relate to employee theft)

Legal Expenses: related to any legal action are not covered. This means if you hire an attorney to respond to charges filed by the employee you thought was stealing, there is no coverage for that legal expense.

Under **GENERAL CONDITIONS:**

Concealment, Misrepresentation or fraud: The insurance is void in any case of fraud by you as it relates to this insurance at any time. It is also void if you or any other insured, at any time, intentionally conceal or misrepresent a material fact concerning:

    a. This insurance,
    b. The covered property,
    c. Your interest in the covered property,
    d. A claim under this insurance. (Same wording in the BOP.)

Records: You must keep records of all covered property so the insurance company can verify the amount of loss. (The BOP. states that the company may examine and audit your books and records as they relate to this policy at any time during the policy period and up to three years afterward).

Consolidation/merger: In the event through consolidation or merger you purchase additional assets from another company, to include more employees and or premises, there is coverage for those additions, if you notify the insurance company within **30 days** of the acquisitions,and you pay any additional premium.

Duties in the event of loss: After you discover a loss or a situation that may result in a loss you must:

    a. Notify the insurance company as soon as possible.
    b. Submit to examination under oath at the request of the insurance company and give them a signed statement of your answers.
    c. Submit a detailed, sworn proof of loss within 120 days.
    d. Cooperate with the insurance company in the investigation and settlement of any claim. (The BOP. policy says the same thing except they require the proof of loss in 60 days).

Some comment about "examination under oath" is in order. This is not to be confused with the fact finding statement that an adjuster or investigator my take to try and determine the facts of the loss. The examination under oath is done when the company questions whether you have documented a loss to their satisfaction, but you still feel that you have a valid claim. It is also done if the company suspects that there may be fraud or other illegal activity involved. The examination is conducted by an attorney, selected and paid by the insurance company and a court reporter to record the proceedings.

Here are some of the more important coverage wordings for this bond policy.

Joint insured:

a. If there are several names in the policy under insured, the first name listed will act for itself and for any other names listed as this insurance is concerned.

b. Notice to one insured or partner is notice to all insureds. This means, if an officer of the company in California is advised of employee theft and fails to act on that notice, and additional theft takes place, there is no coverage for that additional theft even if the main office in Cleveland was never advised about the first theft.

c. An employee of one insured is an employee of every insured.

d. If insurance is cancelled or terminated for any insured, loss sustained is covered if discovered within one year of the termination date.

e. The company will not pay more for one insured's loss than they would pay if there is the same loss that affects other insureds named in the policy.

Legal action against the insurance company: You can not file any legal action against the insurance company involving loss;

a. Unless you have complied with all terms of the insurance policy, and,

b. Unless you waited 90 days after the proof of loss was filed by you to the insurance company; and

c. Unless legal action has been filed within two years from the date you discover the loss. (The BOP. policy does not require a proof of loss before starting legal action).

Liberization: If the company broadens coverage without requiring additional premium within 45 days prior to or during the policy period, the broadened coverage will immediately apply to this insurance. (Same wording in the BOP).

Loss sustained during prior insurance (see above)

Loss covered under this insurance and prior insurance issued by us or any affiliate; If any loss is covered:

a. Partly by this insurance; and
b. Partly by any prior cancelled or terminated insurance issued by any affiliate of the company to you or any predecessor in interest of yours, the most the company will pay is the larger of the amount recoverable under this insurance or the prior insurance.

Non-cumulation of limit of Insurance: Coverage is not cumulative from year to year. This means that if you had carried $50,000 in employee dishonesty coverage for five years with no losses and the six year you sustain a $100,000 loss but your coverage was still $50,000 the most you could recover would be $50,000.

Other insurance: This insurance does not apply to loss recoverable under any other insurance or indemnity. However, if that other insurance is not enough to cover the agreed amount of loss, then this insurance will pay the difference, over the insured's deductible, but will not pay more than the amount of coverage written for this policy.

Policy period: The loss must take place during the policy dates shown or listed in the policy declarations page. In employee theft losses, a theft may begin under one policy date, and other thefts, by the same employee, may take place under another policy date. Sometimes this results in more than one bonding company investigating the loss.

Territory: The policies are in effect for acts committed or events occurring within the United States of America, U. S. Virgin Islands, Puerto Rico, Canal Zone and Canada. The exception to that is a 90 day "extension of coverage" for employees working outside the stated territorial limits.

The remaining sections will be covered under this and other chapters.

Ownership of Property; Interest Covered; In the CR. form it states "The property covered under this insurance is limited to property: a. That you own or hold; or b. For which you are legally liable. However, this insurance is for your benefit only. It provides no rights or benefits to any other person or organization."

Some comments about property that you "hold" or are "legally liable" for should be explained. The above definition is found in the CR 10 00 'Crime Provision' form. The word "hold" can have two meanings. "Hold" can be another word for ownership. In Black's Law Dictionary it states in part "To possess in virtue of a lawful title; as in the expression, common in grants, 'to have and to hold' or in that applied to notes, 'the owner and holder.'"

The word "hold" can also mean that you have something in your possession that belongs to someone else. An example could be that a delivery is attempted at the business address next to yours but no one is there, so the driver ask you to sign for it. You have taken possession of some property that is not yours but will be in your office until the owner returns to his or her office.

Because in the definition the use of the word "or", separates "own" and "hold," my interpretation is that the word "hold" refers to property that belongs to someone else. This is confirmed by two CR. endorsements that are available. The CR 10 07, replaces the ownership of property provision by this wording "to property the insured owns or leases," (rather than coverage for property the insured owns or holds, or for which the insured is legally liable for). Another endorsement CR 10 08, excludes client's property except while on the insured premises. Since there is no mention of the word "client" in the definition in the basic CR 10 00 form, only the wording "property that you hold" I have to conclude the **intent** of the wording "hold" was for property that belonged to the client of the insured. However, since the policy does not state "client," if you have anyone's property that is stolen by an employee under an employee theft policy, there would appear to be coverage under the bond for that property.

In Black's Law Dictionary the definition of b."legally liable" is stated as: Liable under law as interpreted by the courts. It goes on to include "Liability imposed by law or liability which law fixes by contract."

"Legal liability" usually means some form of negligence must be found, or committed by the person before he or she is considered liable. The liability by contract is fairly clear. If you as the employer have a contract, which would include a lease agreement, for a piece of equipment that is owned by someone else and that equipment is stolen or damaged by an employee of yours during the act of theft by the employee, the "Employee Dishonesty Policy" may pay for that loss or damage.

Another example of "legally liable" might be if an employee of yours steals property of a client, and during the investigation it is determined the employer should have known the employee had a history of dishonesty.

From the definition above, the policy states "for your benefit only". This means that if an employee steals property that belongs to another employee or to another company, there is no payment to the person or company that owned the property.

Additionally, should any payment be made for any loss to property that the insured was found to be legally liable for, payment is to the insured not to anyone else.

The Value placed on property depends on what property is involved. Relating to **money** or **cash**, the amount paid is the face value of that money. (This and other property values are discussed in the Adjustment chapter).

There is another form that I have had experience with. This is the **"Employee Dishonesty Coverage, 'schedule' form: CR 00 02."**. This provided the same coverage as the CR 00 01 except it requires that either employees be named with the specific amount of coverage for each employee, or that certain positions be listed with the appropriate amount of coverage for each position.

As the coverage implies, in the proof of loss form the employer **must list an identified employee** as the one they are naming as being responsible for the theft.

There are additional CR. fidelity forms as well as several endorsements available under the CR. policies that can mold coverage to the your situation. Your insurance agent is the individual you should speak with concerning these coverages.

These forms and their endorsements are "standard" policies used by many insurance companies that have their policies sold through independent agents. The governing body or organization that administers these forms is the Insurance Services Organization which we in the business refer to as the "ISO."

Any employer that purchases insurance through agents that use ISO forms will find the same forms regardless of who they buy the insurance from. The cost or premium for a policy, and the amount that an insurance company will go on the risk for, will vary from company to company but that is not the subject of this book.

OTHER BOND FORMS:

I mentioned other bond forms earlier in this chapter. Most of these bond forms are written by carriers that have placed their own wording to better fit their **"market"**. **"Market," refers to the persons or companies that the insurance company believes it has a chance to sell insurance to.** These policies are called **"manuscript policies."**

One example is a large insurance company that specializes in the auto dealer business. Their bond policy has very similar definitions and wordings to the ISO forms. There is one major difference, in that if a partner of the company is responsible for the employee theft, there can still be coverage if he or she did not have controlling interest in the company. You will recall in the ISO forms **any** partner involvement excluded coverage under the bond.

There are additional crime forms that have come into the market. One company refers to their policy as **"Executive Protection Policy"**, another calls its policy **"Crime Guard"**. These policies place all crime coverage under one type of policy heading, sort of like a combined, blanket or umbrella for crime losses. Many of the policy exclusions and conditions are similar to the CR. policy, but there are some differences.

- One large difference concerns an employee's past history. In the CR. policy any past dishonest history voids coverage of that employee under the new coverage. Under these combined forms if the past theft, fraud or dishonesty was not over $25,000 the employee could **still** be covered under the current policy.

- In the CR. and BOP. policies the employee must benefit from the theft, that wording **is not written** in the combined forms.
- There is no wording concerning "manifest intent' required.
- The discovery period is not one year as in the CR policy, but either 60 or 90 days depending on what combined policy is read.
- Employees of any temporary agency or other employment contractor are still covered, but the combined forms become **excess** over any policy that the employment agency carries on that employee. This means the employment agency coverage would respond to your loss first. If there was coverage under that policy, your employee dishonesty policy would not respond, unless it was needed as excess or secondary coverage.
- In the **"Crime Guard"** form volunteers and students gaining work experience are covered.
- In the **"Crime Guard"** form written notice of loss must be given in 90 days, not 120 as in the other forms.

The final policy forms that I will mention are known as **"Janitorial Service"** or **"Business Service Bond."** The main differences in these forms as compared to other employee dishonesty coverage are that;

- The loss or theft has to take place **in or on the premises** of the client that your company does service for.
- The theft must be during the **regular servicing** of the client's premises.
- There has to be a **conviction** of the employee responsible for the theft, which means there must be police involvement. This is not true of the CR. or BOP. or the manuscript forms discussed above, unless another crime is thought to be the cause of loss, such as Burglary, Robbery or non employee Theft.

As you can see from these different forms, it is very important that you the insured, provide all information to the insurance agent so the proper form and coverage amount can be written for your company.

Finally, it is also very important that whatever employee coverage you and your agent decide is best for you, that you place any crime coverage such as **"Money and Securities"** or **"Theft, Destruction and Disappearance"** with the same company. (This may not be necessary with the combined crime forms discussed above). The reason for this is that there may be losses where it cannot be determined whether it is an employee dishonesty loss or some other crime loss.

CASE HISTORY: I was called to investigate a theft of several laptop computers from a Washington DC. real estate developer. The insured's offices were located in a medium high rise office building. The doors leading to the office of the insured had locks, and there was never any indication of forcible entry. The laptops were used by several key employees. There was no history of theft by any of the employees. The offices were cleaned several nights a week by a separate janitorial contractor. In speaking to the management of the building, they could not provide any strong information that would indicate any employees of the contractor were involved. In my opinion the loss was probably from an outside non employee type person or persons, but difficult to prove without police polygraphs. (I think the employees of the cleaning service placed the laptops in the large trash cans they carried around during the cleaning of the rooms).

If the insured did not have coverage for both employee theft and other crime coverage with the same company there is a question whether the company would have made a payment. Since the loss was covered under one or the other polices and both were with the same company the carrier knew they would have to pay the claim. The question was under which policy. They paid it under the crime policy, which carried a deductible.

HOW MUCH COVERAGE SHOULD YOU CARRY:

I have reviewed a **"formula"** used by two insurance carriers that write considerable fidelity coverage to determine how much coverage their client should carry. Here is the formula:

1. Enter the firm's total current assets (cash, deposits, securities, receivables, goods on hand etc.) $ _____
   a. Enter the value of goods on hand (raw materials, materials in process, finished merchandise or products) $ _____
   b. Enter 5% of a. $ _____
   c. Enter current assets less goods on hand, i.e. the difference between 1. and 1-a. $ _____
   d. Enter 20% of c. $ _____
2. Enter annual gross sales or income $ _____
   a. Enter 10% of 2. $ _____

   This is the firms dishonesty exposure index. $ _____
   This is the suggested minimum amount of insurance. $ _____

There is a four column chart **(appendix 1)** that has the range of your dishonesty exposure from $25,000 to $500,000,000 on the two columns on the left, and the amount of suggested coverage in the two columns on the right. The minimum suggested limit is $15,000 and the maximum is $3,000,000.

For example if your index was between $750,000 and $1,000,000 the range of coverage would be $100,000 to $125,000.

If your index was $11,425.000 to $15,000,000 the range of coverage would be $700,000 to $800,000.

For greater understanding of the **formula** and the **suggested minimum amount of insurance** I suggest you contact your insurance agent.

This chapter has summarized many of the employee dishonesty coverages available today. Now we discuss what to do when you "discover" an employee theft loss.

Chapter Five

Discovery

What to Do When You Have Employee Theft

When the existence of an employee dishonesty or theft loss comes to the attention of **YOU**, the employer (insured), the word ""**discovery"** is used to describe that event.

Neither the CR 00 01 or the optional coverage in the BOP. policy define what constitutes discovery. However, both forms state that coverage is cancelled as to any "employee": a. immediately upon discovery by:

1. You; or
2. Any of your partners, officers or directors not in collusion with the "employee"; of any dishonest act committed by that "employee" whether before or after becoming employed by you.

So to paraphrase, **"discovery" can be defined to occur when an employee dishonesty act comes to the attention of you or any of your officers, partners, or directors not in collusion with the "employee."**

The word "You" and "Your"in the General Crime Provisions refer to the Named Insured shown in the declarations section of the policy. This section lists who or what business or entity is being insured.

As stated previously, but worth repeating, any officer of the main corporation or other "insured" under the word insured in the declaration page qualifies as someone that is responsible for notifying management once they become aware of employee dishonesty. To do otherwise could cause monetary disaster for the insured.

CASE HISTORY: *The employee of one of many insureds listed in the declarations page of the bond policy stole quite a bit of money through several schemes. The main insured was a large hospital. These losses went on for many years. Close to the end, when the employee felt that others working with her may have become aware of monetary problems in this employee's department, the thief confided with the current president of the auxiliary, that came under the Foundation Corp. of the hospital, that she had stolen some money, but that she had replaced it. The president of the auxiliary did not check to see if the money had indeed been replaced. She did ask the employee if there had been any more theft, to which the employee said no. Nothing more was done by that president. The loss was not "discovered" until four months later. After an investigation and the information from the president of the auxiliary was verified, the bonding company felt that they could deny coverage because the **insured did not comply with "Duties in the event of loss" which states under (c) Submit a detailed, sworn proof of loss within 120 days.***

It was the bonding company's position that the president of the auxiliary was an officer of the insured. If that was true, then "notice to one (insured) is notice to all (insureds)." With the auxiliary president not notifying management right away, by the time the loss was "discovered" there was no way the insured could submit the "proof of loss" within 120 days. Therefore the insured was in policy violation. I did not agree with the company's position for two reasons. First, I felt that the auxiliary was not a legal entity (not listed as an insured). If not a legal entity, then the president of the auxiliary was not an officer under the bond. Secondly, I felt that the policy wording, under the "duties in the event of loss" did not state that the bonding company could deny coverage if the insured did not comply with this section of the policy. (I discuss this and my position in Chapter 6, Adjustment). Eventually the insurance company agreed to provide coverage because of the lack of a "legal entity" status.

There is no wording in these policies that allows "You" to designate someone that is to receive notice of any employee theft problem or occurrence. The exception to that is under the CR 00 16 and CR 00 17 which are the **"Public Employee Dishonesty Coverage Forms."** These forms will allow discovery to extend to **any official or employee authorized to manage, govern or control your employees, of any dishonest act committed by that "employee" whether before or after becoming employed by you.**

In the aforementioned definition that had wording "not in Collusion with the employee", that refers to any officers that may be in a conspiracy with the employee. There is a big reason for this wording. In any situation where you have a trusted corporate officer working with an employee to steal from the employer, the results can be devastating to the employer.

---

*CASE HISTORY: Years ago there was a very successful auto dealer in Washington, DC. The owner had hired an experienced general manager and made him a vice president. The dealership was in the market for a new Finance and Insurance Manager (in the industry they are called F & I managers.) This general manager hired a past associate of his from a previous dealer. Together they embezzled over $70,000 from the dealership through a variety of schemes. If the discovery started with the time **this officer** had notice of a theft there would have been no covered loss. This would be against the purpose of the employee theft coverage.*

(Had this vice president been a partner, it is quite possible that there would have been no coverage for this loss. Therefore it is crucial that the owner of a company be very careful who is made a partner in that company).

PROCEDURES AFTER DISCOVERY:

It is my intent through this book to assist the employer in not only understanding all aspects of employee theft, but to also make recommendations that will benefit the employer. These are based on over two decades of employee theft investigations. These suggestions are not taken from the works of other authorities on this subject, but rather from discoveries in actual conversations and meetings with insurance agents, accountants, employers and the results of experiences in working with these groups. These suggestions are made to provide the employer with not only what I believe to be the best way to resolve a problem, but to also decrease the insured's chances of having legal difficulties from these situations. These suggestions will be quite evident in the remainder of this chapter and remaining chapters as well.

It is important that once discovery is made by or to the proper person that quick and correct action be taken. If there is notice of a loss but no specific employee can be identified or the employee thought to be responsible no longer works at the company, the police should be contacted as well as your insurance agent and company attorney. If the theft is from one occurrence, as much as possible, the area where the theft originated from should be kept clear in case the police want to have the crime lab process the scene. You should prepare a schedule of who worked where, and start gathering your loss documentation. This will be covered in the next chapter.

Your responsibilities differ when you have a loss and you are aware of who is responsible. For purpose of this discussion, I will assume that employee theft was discovered, and there is no doubt who did it. This confirmation could be from direct observation from an officer of the company or from a surveillance camera. Or as a result of the employee making an error in his scheme that allowed the theft to be uncovered. It could also come from the employee making a voluntary confession himself.

The company attorney and accountant should be contacted as well as the insurance agent for the bonding company. The insurance company may have a specific policy on how to work with an employee involved theft, but you cannot always wait for them to respond. Sometimes days or a week or more can go by before someone from the insurance company contacts you. Meanwhile, depending on the circumstances, you may have one of the following situations.

If the employee does not know that he or she has been discovered, you want to make it impossible for that employee to steal anymore. As I discussed earlier, once there is "discovery," all future losses from that employee are not covered.

However, you want to have control of the situation so you can obtain as much information from the employee as possible before termination. **The ultimate goal here is to terminate the employee from your company as soon as possible, but you want to have everything in place before you act on that termination.** For example you may need time to gather some of the documents you will present to the employee in the termination meeting. You may need time to have the right person conduct such a meeting. You may want to begin the process of freezing the bank accounts of the employee, so you can recover money before it is withdrawn by the employee. (This requires the hiring of an attorney and obtaining a court order which will enable you to freeze the funds in the employee's account before she has the opportunity to withdraw them.)

If the employee is working in the office and that is the source of the theft, you can make changes that will make it difficult for the employee to continue that theft.

CASE HISTORY: *There was a Doctor's office where the office manager stole $40,000 in six months, by writing checks to herself from the accounts payable checkbook. (This will be covered in great detail in Management Controls, Chapter 10). If the employer wanted to keep her in the office for a few days he could have simply denied her access to the checkbook.*

If a manager is suspected of stealing deposits, make a corporate decision for two people to write up and make the deposits. I am not talking about having to wait for weeks before a termination, just a few days until you receive proper instructions or are in position to regain control.

WHEN EMPLOYEES CONFESS:

The other situation occurs when it is impossible to make changes to both safeguard your assets from additional theft and keep the employee there at the same time. In this case the employee should be brought into the company conference room or private office where conversations cannot be heard by other employees outside of the office. As much documentation concerning the discovery of this employee 's dishonesty should be brought out and the employee confronted. If the documentation is unrefutable, the employee will usually admit to his or her guilt.

It is imperative that you remember several important points when dealing with an employee in this situation. You may be very angry, especially if this was an employee well liked by the company. If this employee had been in your employ for many years and had received awards for his or her effort, the involvement of this employee will be especially hard to take.

You must remember that this is not the time to be yelling at the employee and making comments such as "How could you do this to us." You need to understand that obtaining information at this time is more important than accusations. Remember:

- **The employee may be willing to say and do more now, than he or she will tomorrow.** You should understand that if the employee has been confronted with cold facts of his or her theft, he knows he has been caught. At this time he is thinking; Am I going to lose my job?, What do I tell my family?, Will I go to jail?
- Another important point **is that even though this person stole from you, he still has "rights."** It is illegal to harass or physically or mentally abuse the employee.
- **You cannot force the employee to cooperate**, and it is not wise to make any promises to the employee about criminal charges or discussions about paying the money back prior to a properly completed confession.

If the employee wants an attorney or wants to leave the office without cooperating, you must let him go. You can tell him that he is terminated as of this date. You may have a termination letter typed up with wording that protects you and the employee. This is something for your corporate attorney to assist you with.

If the employee wants to cooperate, then the proper procedure calls for there to be at least two adult senior members of your staff in attendance during this meeting. By implementing this plan you will have support for your version of what went on in that meeting. (I have been involved in a few isolated cases where the employee said that he or she was forced to cooperate or confess, or that promises were made that the employer later wanted to take back).

I have always recommended that, whenever possible, a written or recorded confession be taken. If it is in writing, it should be in the handwriting of the employee. This confession should be taken by someone who can ask probing questions but handle the matter in a business like fashion. An attorney, private investigator, or risk consultant is best qualified for that position.

At this time the employee is at a disadvantage. He may be more cooperative now in providing details on how long the theft has been going on, the amount he believes he stole, how he accomplished the theft, and if any one else was involved. You will also want to know what was done with the money. Were any purchases made? If there are any bank accounts, you may want the bank names and account numbers. You also want to add whether the employee's spouse (assuming the person is married) or any other relative was aware of the theft, (reasons for this will be covered in Chapter 7, Subrogation, Recovery and Restitution).

Remember, once the employee seeks and retains an attorney you are not allowed to have any further contact with that now ex-employee without the attorney's permission. This permission he or she will not normally give.

The wording at the end of the confession is very important. I suggest something along these lines: "I gave this confession freely without mental or physical abuse or duress. I have not been given or made any promises concerning employment, civil litigation, criminal prosecution or restitution".

Both the employee and anyone that was in the meeting should sign the confession. The employee should also be given a copy of the confession and sign that he has received it.

Anytime you are working with an employee theft loss the situation is not very pleasant. Perhaps the most difficult situation is where the loss is thought to be by employee, and you know the person or persons responsible are still employed by you, but you cannot identify the thief. In this situation you must be extremely cautious in not making accusations that may turn out to be incorrect. Of course, you as the employer, want to identify the thief as quickly as possible. But there are "Management Controls" that can be placed into effect almost immediately so the risk of a similar loss is lessened. Making the wrong accusation could result in a lawsuit that could cost you more than what you may have lost in the employee theft. Terminating the wrong employee could result in a very expensive wrongful discharge suit that could dwarf the employee theft loss. Because of these very real concerns it is important that you follow these guidelines as well as the instructions from your corporate attorney, bonding company, and the police or States Attorney.

Besides the previous comments concerning what you can and cannot do in a termination meeting with the employee, there are three other actions by you the employer that must be discussed.

LIE DETECTOR EXAM:

The first takes place when you, the employer, do not know which current employee is responsible for the theft. You hope by having all employees submit to a polygraph exam (lie detector) that you can determine from the results who may be responsible. In the State of Maryland it is illegal to require an employee to take the polygraph exam or to use the employee's refusal to take the exam as an admission of guilt and then terminate the employment of that employee.

If the employee volunteers to take an exam, that is permissible but you better have that permission in writing and have it properly witnessed. You also cannot use the need to submit to a polygraph exam as a condition of hiring someone. There are some exceptions, and that will be covered in Chapter nine, Management Controls, Pre-Employment.

You as the employer cannot force the employees to submit to drug testing in hopes that finding someone with a positive result, will help you draw the conclusion that they have a drug habit and need to steal to support that habit. Of course you should check with the regulations in your state and how those regulations pertain to your profession or business.

COMMENTS TO OTHER EMPLOYEES, AND PROSPECTIVE EMPLOYERS:

What you say to other employees about another employee's dishonesty depends on several things. If there is some question as to who is involved then no specific names should be discussed with other employees.

CASE HISTORY: There was a large beer distributor in Washington D.C.. Investigation determined that someone was shorting the cases of beer that were being loaded on the delivery trucks from the main shipping point. By checking schedules in relation to the days the loading was short, there were five people who could be responsible for the theft. The employer considered firing all five employees but he was talked out of that action. If he had done that he would have faced a wrongful discharge suit by all five employees, because the loss could not be pinned down to one person and there was insufficient evidence to prove a conspiracy. Firing all five men would have been a major mistake from a legal standpoint.

*What was done however was to tighten controls and to send a general letter to **all employees** that the company was aware that there had been a shortage of beer loading on the trucks and that when the company found out who was responsible they would be prosecuted.*

I am a firm believer that employees should know when they are hired, that the company will prosecute those responsible for theft. Placing this type wording on the employment contract, which usually requires an employee's signature, is an example of notifying employees of company intentions.

Also company meetings or literature disbursed to the employees on a periodic basis are also suggested ways of making sure employees constantly know the company's stance on a very important matter.

If appropriate and practical, signs could be posted warning employees that employee theft will result in termination and prosecution. These signs work well in warehouse or factory locations.

In the circumstance where it is clear who is responsible for the theft, I still believe that only employees that have a need to know should be made aware of the situation. I state this for several reasons. First you want to have as much cooperation from the employee as possible for reasons that were discussed above. If the general work force is told about the specific employee involved, someone is going to contact that employee to verify what they have heard. At this point the employee is not only embarrassed by the conversation, but will become defensive and possibly angry. He or she will probably not cooperate further with the employer, and may even try to take the position that he wants to fight the charges. **Remember, even if you think you have the law on your side, there is always someone who will try to get a court of law to see it otherwise.**

Additionally until that court finds the employee guilty you should not broadcast that they are guilty.

There is no need to create a situation where the employee tries to prove a libel or slanderous action against you. Granted you may have a confession, but what if that employee retains an attorney and tries to show that the confession was coerced. A guilty verdict in criminal court is protection for the employer for any allegations of libel or slander, but what if your board of directors or corporate officers feel that you should not prosecute? Perhaps they feel that a public criminal trial is embarrassing to the corporation.

I have had several insureds refuse to pursue criminal action because they felt the public awareness would be detrimental to their image. What if the States Attorney does not feel that the amount of loss, or facts make it practical to pursue a criminal trial? As the one who sustained the loss you are the victim. You do not want to do anything to alter that position.

Finally I want to discuss what an employer should say to prospective employers when they call and inquire on the job performance of someone they (the prospective employer) are considering hiring. There is nothing in the insurance or bond policy to instruct the insured on what to say. In reviewing news letters from accountants or insurance agents, I have not read where employers received instructions on explaining what they should do or say in this situation. Yet, I have had a number of employers ask me what they should say. Sometimes I ask them how they will handle inquires in this area. Some employers would comment differently depending on whether the employee had confessed to or was caught in a dishonest act, as contrasted to the situation where the insured was never able to prove an employee's guilt. (This could arise when employee theft was discovered after the employee thought to be responsible had left the company). Obviously an employer's exposure for slander is greater in the latter versus the former situation.

Even in those cases where there is no doubt who is responsible for the theft, my instructions to the employer are to reveal to the prospective employer only the dates that the employee worked, and what her duties were. If the prospective employer asks why the employee was terminated you simply say that you cannot discuss reasons for dismissal. If the person asks if you would rehire the employee, you can say that you would not rehire them. (Some employers have advised me that they do not respond either way if asked whether they would rehire.) To be safe, follow what your attorney says.

My approach is to protect you the employer. I do not recommend that you say anything that could come back to cause you legal problems. Remember unless there has been a criminal conviction of that employee, he or she is still legally innocent of any theft. Saying that you would not rehire someone is not a slanderous statement, yet it should give the prospective employer some insight into who they want to hire.

I do not think employers realize how easy it is for someone to start a defamation of character suit against a former employer. Insurance companies know, because they make the settlements on these cases. They know how a situation can be turned around to the employee's advantage.

CASE HISTORY: Several years ago I represented an insurance company that wrote the employee dishonesty coverage for many auto dealers in the Maryland area. One of these dealers had an employee theft loss which I investigated. The evidence pointed to one of their employees, but he did not confess and the employer did not want to pursue the matter through criminal court. The employee was terminated.

When I became involved the employee was already working for a competitor dealer. The investigation clearly showed his involvement. The competitor dealer was also insured by the same insurance company. I asked the claims department of the insurance company if someone should advise the new dealer about the person they had hired. The home office of the insurance company said that no comments could be made about this employee to his new employer. They were worried about legal problems that could have been started by the employee if he was fired by his new employer based on the comment made by the insurance company.

Some employers, however, feel that they have an obligation to warn other employers about who they are hiring. This can be a big mistake.

CASE HISTORY: I am currently working with an auto dealer where the employee has verbally admitted to stealing from the employer. No written confession was obtained. The employee has refused to cooperate with my office. The employer does not want to pursue this in the criminal court system because of the bad publicity. Yet the manager of the dealership advised that if any employers call about this employee he will tell them what he (the employee) did. I explained to the manager why that

could cause a legal problem for the dealership. There is no con-
fession, there is no admission of guilt to the bonding company,
nor is there criminal conviction.

EMPLOYER LIABILITY LAW:

In State of Maryland there has been a newly enacted law that is to protect the employer from liability when they disclose information about an employee or former employee. This is House Bill 597. I enclose a copy of this bill **(appendix 2)** and it's final wording as a Law in Maryland 1996.

What bothers me about this law is that although its intent is to protect the employer who acts in "Good Faith", the definition of "Good Faith" is not part of the law. Black's Law Dictionary defines "Good Faith" in part as "an intangible and abstract quality with no technical meaning or statutory definition"..In common usage this term is ordinarily used to describe that state of mind denoting honesty of purpose, freedom from intention to defraud. . . .

The law does not protect the employer who acts with malice toward the employee or who intentionally or recklessly discloses false information about the employee. Lets take the manager of the auto dealer who felt obligated to tell prospective employers of the actions of the employee. If the manager tells that the employee stole from the dealership, is that an accurate statement? The employee supposedly verbally confessed, but there is no written confession. The employee has not been found guilty in a court of law. As we know from recently publicized national criminal cases no matter how compelling the evidence, a person is still innocent until proven guilty in a court of law. Bearing this in mind would the comments made by the manager be of acting in "Good Faith" or acting in "Malice"? You should draw your own conclusions, or consult with your attorney. Your attorney will be able to research if your own state has a law similar to Maryland's.

As of this writing I am not aware of anyone challenging this law or the interpretation of wording in the law. However, sometime someone will challenge this law. All I say to you the employer, is that you do not have to expose yourself or your company to legal interpretations or needless lawsuits. My suggestions are clear, easy to follow, and can still provide prospective employers with proper information so they can make an informed decision without causing legal concerns for you the past employer.

Now that "discovery" of the loss is over, and you have information on how to work with the "employee" and "prospective employers," you turn your attention to the adjustment of your loss.

Chapter Six

The Adjustment Process

The adjustment or claim part of an employee dishonesty loss begins when the insurance company that underwrites the bond coverage receives information from either the insured directly, or from the insured's agent that an employee theft loss is thought to have taken place.

The insured or employer normally contacts the agent who will either take information over the telephone on what is known as a "crime loss" form, or if the insurance company has a direct reporting procedure, refer the insured directly to the claims office of the insurance company.

Depending on the insurance company's procedures, the claim supervisor, assigned to control the investigation, will do one of two things once the insurance or bonding company receives the loss information. This action centers around what is referred to as a **"Fidelity Proof of Loss" (appendix 3)** which must be completed by the insured before any investigation, outside of preliminary meetings with the insured, can take place.

Some insurance companies will require that the supervisor send the form, with a cover letter, to the insured and ask for the form to be completed, then returned to the claims supervisor who will assign the loss for investigation. Other insurance company procedures will require the supervisor to assign the loss immediately for investigation, and allow the person assigned the investigation to take the proof of loss to the insured for its completion.

An explanation of what "a **"Proof of Loss"** and **"Fidelity Proof of Loss"**are and how they differ is important for your understanding of the adjustment of an employee theft loss. The "Proof of Loss" document is a pre-worded document that has blank areas on the form where the specific information about the date, time, and type loss can be written in. Under a standard property policy that covers the insured for damage by fire, wind, freezing, etc. or under crime coverage (excluding employee theft), the form will have a section on the right side that allows for the adjuster or the insured to write in the amount of the loss, any deductible that applies and the net claim amount.

There is considerable wording in the **"Proof"** (as the industry refers to it) that concerns rights and non-waiver of those rights of the insured and or the insurance company. However, it is not the purpose of this chapter to explain the form in it's entirety, only those sections that have a familiarity or difference from the "**Fidelity Proof"**. There is a **"subrogation clause"** that states the insurance company has the right to collect from any other person or company that may be responsible for the loss amount that is paid to the insured under this policy for this loss. The document has a place for a Notary Public and insured's signature. There is also wording on some insurance company forms that states any false or incorrect information submitted for the purpose of defrauding the insurance company can be considered a crime.

After the adjuster completes his or her adjustment, the form is completed, sent or given to the insured for signature and Notary Seal and then submitted to the insurance company for acceptance or rejection. This acceptance or rejection will be based on the supporting documentation that was submitted previously or with the proof of loss at time of submission.

The industry uses "Proofs" because it is a legal document which summarizes the loss and claim information. It also verifies the amount the insured is submitting as their loss and claim. Finally the proof along with a copy of a paid draft or check from the insurance company can be used by that insurance company to collect under "Subrogation" (chapter 7).

The adjustment of an employee dishonesty loss is different than any other property or crime loss and adjustment. Here the "Fidelity Proof of Loss" form is used. This bond "Proof" must be completed by the insured (employer) before any investigation is done to prove or disprove employee theft. The purpose of this form is to protect the bonding company and its representatives from any liability claims that could arise from the employee thought by the employer to be responsible for any theft. The form has a section where the insured fills in the date of "discovery" (chapter 5), and when the loss was reported to the agent or the bonding company, and who the insured feels is involved. If the policy does not require that a specific employee be identified, and if the employer is not sure who is responsible for the theft the word **"unidentified"** can be entered.

If the employee is **"identified"**, the dates of employment, position and some personal information about the employee are to be added. The form also has a section on the left side of the page where the insured is to list the amount of the loss by dates showing each amount from each date and on the right side where any credits can be deducted. These credits could be salary, retirement money or money paid back by the employee. (States may have different laws on what salaries or retirement monies can be held back from the employee. Please check with your CPA or attorney for current law in your state). The credits are deducted from the claim amount and a final or net amount is reached. The form requires that an officer of the insured or employer sign at the bottom and there must always be a Notary Public Seal. This is done because the bonding company wants to verify that it is the employer who is alleging a specific employee was dishonest, not the insurance company.

Most policy wording requires that the sworn "Proof" be submitted to the insurance company within 120 days from the date you discover the loss and notify the insurance company. This is very important since failure to do this or any of the other **"duties"** may result in the company denying coverage. Although the policy wording in this section does not actually state that the company will deny coverage if this provision is not followed, I know that insurance companies have denied claims because of the insured's failure to comply with the wording in this section of the policy. The actual wording is found in the CRIME GENERAL PROVISIONS on the CR 10 00 , it reads as follows:

Duties in the event of loss: After you discover a loss or a situation that may result in loss of, or loss from damage to, Covered Property you must:

    a. Notify us as soon as possible,
    b. Submit to examination under oath at our request and give us a signed statement of your answers,

c. **Give us a detailed, sworn proof of loss within 120 days,**
d. **Cooperate with us in the investigation and settlement of any claim.**

There are court cases where companies have been successful in denying coverage due to the insured's failure to perform one or more of the duties listed. However, in Maryland these denials have been in "auto cases" not "employee dishonesty". Whether a company can sustain a denial will depend on the actions of the insured and how they relate to the loss. Nonetheless, the possibility of a denial in this area of coverage is there. Even if the insurance company is not successful in that denial, it will cost your company the loss of use of any money that would have otherwise been paid until the case is adjudicated. Plus the legal fees you may incur to oppose the denial are probably not reimbursable regardless of the outcome. The bottom line is, you do not want to give the insurance company any reason to consider denial of coverage. You want to comply with all policy wording. Your policy will have wording similar to this. Please check with your agent so you have a thorough understanding of your policy.

You may recall in the "discovery " chapter, I commented about a loss where the insurance company was considering denial based on the fact that an officer, of an auxiliary arm of the insured listed along with many insureds on the declaration page of the policy, failed to report knowledge that an employee theft had taken place.

The insurance company felt that if the company had not complied with the **"duties in the event of loss"** section that denial of the loss was an option. I voiced my position that nowhere in this section of the policy does it state what the company will do if the insured does not comply with those instructions. Yet in other sections of the same policy, phrases such as "we will not pay for loss," or "this insurance is void in any case of". . . . are found. Since these policies are **"unilateral"**, meaning that the insured has no say in the wording of the policy, it is my opinion that if the insurance company wanted to deny coverage because the insured failed to respond according to the "duties" section, the insurance company should have stated that. Instead it reads **"you must.."** and goes on from there, never stating what happens if you don't respond. This position was voiced to the insurance carrier's supervisor involved in that case. He did not agree with me, and referred to the information supplied by the attorney that offered his opinion on what the company options were. However, as I stated above, no court has, as of this writing, denied coverage on a bond loss based on the insured's failure to comply with this section of the policy.

Normally only experienced claims people are used to investigate employee theft claims, because these losses can be complex and have the potential for legal problems for the insurance company if not handled correctly. If the insurance company has access to someone that has an accounting background to go along with claim experience, that individual should receive the assignment. Most of these losses involve loss of money and there can be a need to understand a financial or profit and loss statement.

Your insurance agent or claims supervisor will ask for the name and telephone number of the contact person in your employment. This person should be a company officer who has the most knowledge of what took place. The investigator assigned to your claim will speak only with that contact person until you provide other people who need to be contacted so your loss can be properly investigated. The investigator may take a recorded statement from the person you decide is the contact person. Other statements or interviews may be taken as well, so all pertinent information can be obtained.

The statements are not depositions, but rather are fact finding missions. Personal information about the person giving the interview will be asked in the event such person were to leave the employer, or area, so there would be some information on how to contact the interviewee. This could be important if there were a need for the person to testify at a trial on the theft.

It should be noted that although the statements are not depositions they can be entered as evidence in a trial. They can be used to either help refresh the memory of the witness, or impeach his or her testimony if there is a significant change in what was recorded in the statement versus what is testified to in trial.

If the loss is one where there is no question that it is employee theft and the identity of the person responsible is known, the company will usually want complete copies of the employee's personal file. There is information in the file that the insurance company can use during the adjustment portion of the loss and if there is a payment under the bond, in the "recovery" or "subrogation" phase as well.

The employer will be asked to provide as much information as possible on what they believe is the documentation to support the loss. The extent of the documentation will depend on the type of employee theft loss, the length of time the theft was thought to be going on, and the amounts taken during this theft.

I have been involved in many investigations/ thefts where the complexities were such that the insured retained a CPA firm or other consultant to reconstruct the loss. Please be aware that under most insurance coverage there is no reimbursement for the expense associated with this consult. These experts can submit invoices for fees that can reach into five figures, so the insured has to weigh the cost of this service in relation to the extent of the loss.

CASE HISTORY: A large medical facility sustained an employee loss that went on for over six years. They retained a CPA firm to audit the loss. The work done was excellent and amounted to several notebooks filled with computer generated schedules and breakdown of charges that made up the loss. The CPA firm charged over $15,000 for their services. The amount of loss was over $100,000. Could the insured have proven their loss without the CPA's work? The facility had in house accountants that could have completed the work, but consider what facility work they would not be doing while the staff worked on this project. This would be a loss of business that is not covered under the bond policy. Should the insurance company have retained a firm, at company expense, to perform the work that was done? The insurance company cannot prove your loss or claim for you. All they can do is assist in suggesting what documents will go to prove what the insured thinks is the loss.

It is not uncommon for an accounting firm to be retained by the bonding company to check the loss. What that usually means is that after the insured or employer submits all documentation, the firm retained by the insurance company reviews the documents and determines whether all or part of the loss can be considered for payment under the coverage. In many losses the accountant does what a trained investigator can do but the CPA works faster, has the computer software to show the results in a professional manner and more importantly can testify as an expert to what was and was not proven. In large losses the investigator and insurance company retained CPA work well together for the main focus of determining what part of the loss should be covered.

The more paperwork and documentation involved, the longer it takes for the loss to be examined and as a result reported with recommendations. Sometimes however, the amount involved is not a fair representation on how complex the loss was. I have had a loss for $70,000 that had so many documents that many boxes were needed to hold the supporting paperwork. I have also had losses over $200,000 where there were less than ten checks involved.

The bonding companies want to close the adjustment of these claims as quickly as possible, but some losses are more difficult to confirm. My approach has always been to recommend only that amount of loss that could stand up in a court of law. In cases where the identity of the responsible employee is known and if the amount is over $10,000 (there is no set minimum limit) the States Attorney would probably like to look into the case. This assumes the employer wants to pursue the case through the criminal court system as well as file a claim against the bonding company. If any of the claim information is so unclear as to whether or not that specific portion of a loss can be attributed to the employee in question, a good defense attorney for the employee would be able to refute the allegation in court. Thus, I would not recommend that the questionable amount be made a part of the loss. Additionally the insured may not have sufficient back up documents to prove that one or more transactions were part of the theft. These too, I would not recommend. Companies may not always agree with what their investigator suggests but it is a good basis from which to work. The clearer the documentation, the faster the claim can be presented to the insurance company and payment made.

Usually the larger the loss, the longer the theft goes on, and or the amount of documents on the claim, will determine the length of time the adjustment takes. It is not uncommon for losses to take nine months or longer for completion. Some losses are easy to document to the investigator and in turn the insurance company. Losses of cash from deposits or checks from the checking account are not difficult to track and prove. Losses that involve inventory loss or money taken through fraudulent vouchers or invoices are more difficult to confirm.

The investigator will gather all your documents and ask questions that will help him or her understand what happened. What is usually done is to obtain some preliminary information about what the facts are, then take a statement from the employer or the individual that the employer had asked to cooperate with the investigator.

The reason for a statement, besides what was discussed earlier, is that this will allow a review of the insured's explanation of what was done in his or her words. Sometimes it is easier to understand how the theft was accomplished when you can hear or read it from the insured.

Questions normally asked will be:

- Why do you think you have an employee theft loss?
- When did the loss first come to the attention of an officer or employer?
- What was done?
- Whom do you think is responsible for the loss, and why?
- How large is the loss and what documentation do you have to prove the loss?

If the information received by the employer seems to focus on one specific employee, a number of questions will be asked about that employee.

- When did he or she start work there?
- What background check was completed?
- Is there an application for employment?
- Is there a question on the form about past criminal history?
- Have any past thefts from this employee been brought to attention previously?.

If you have read the previous chapters you will know the reason for some of these questions. You must realize that although the insurance companies want to pay all of the documented amount you have lost as a result of employee dishonesty, and it is the job of the investigator and adjuster to assist you in that regard, the companies must also determine if there have been any policy violations that would exclude coverage. By these type questions three agendas are met: the amount of the loss claimed by the insured, possible identification of the employee (s) who may be responsible for that loss, and the discovery of any violations that would exclude coverage. The adjuster/investigator is the one who can best obtain all these answers.

You have read the word "documentation" several times in this chapter. This refers to whatever the insured has, to prove a theft has taken place. Sometimes the documentation is very easy and clear such as videos of employee theft taking place, or cancelled checks showing the employee's name as payee. Other times the back up is muddled and requires detailed investigation. Usually the documents are in some form of paper transactions. This is called a "paper trail", and it can sometimes be a very long trail, full of difficulties for everyone. Your cooperation is needed and required. You may have to supply hundreds of pages of documents in order to prove your claim.

If cash was taken through fraudulent use of checks, invoices, credit cards, or deposits, then copies of bank statements, cancelled checks, and business or transaction back up are necessary in order to prove that a loss to you has taken place. If the loss is of an inventory item you will be asked to prove that you had received the item and what its value is.

Remember, besides all the coverage concerns discussed throughout the previous chapters, it is necessary to show that you, the insured, lost money or lost inventory that you were owner of or responsible for, and that the employee received a financial benefit over and above his or her normal pay. This last point is not required in the combined forms.

When I ask for documentation, I want to be able to have that information confirm the loss, have it point to a specific employee and have it stand up in criminal court under the best cross examination by the attorney for the defendant. However, it does not always work that way. Sometimes you have information that points to employee theft but you do not know which employee is responsible. Sometimes the insured claims a loss but cannot prove that it was employee theft.

An explanation of these are in order. In an earlier chapter I discussed the theft of beer from the delivery trucks before the trucks left the warehouse. By the information obtained from the insured they proved employee theft, but we could not narrow down the number of employees that could be responsible. The loss was under $10,000 so it was not a case that justified extensive legal fees from depositions and court appearances to try and point the loss on one person.

An example of where the insured was not able to prove their claim can be seen from this case.

CASE HISTORY: *A local branch of a regional bank discovered that a very expensive computer used in bank audits was discovered missing. Investigation determined that although the computer had been signed out by a specific employee, the record keeping of the sign in and out sheet was not kept up well. Additionally the room where this computer was kept allowed easy access by non-employee type individuals, such as vendors and janitorial services. The police became involved. They felt that there was insufficient evidence to focus on one employee. They agreed that non-employee types could have had access to the computer storage. There was no confession from the employee the bank wanted to focus on. The end result was that no payment was made.*

Do you recall in an earlier chapter where I wrote of the importance of having all crime coverage with the same insurance company and that you should carry crime coverage for other losses besides employee theft. This company did not carry that other coverage. Had they carried crime coverage that covers property stolen by someone other than an employee, they would probably have had coverage for this loss.

After the insured submits the "Fidelity Proof Of Loss" as well as sufficient documents to confirm that an employee loss has taken place, the company investigator will begin contact with the employee named in the proof. If no employee is named, and if that is not a policy violation, the company investigator may assist you in trying to determine which employee could have been responsible for the theft. Some questions asked may be focused on who may fit the qualities of someone that could be responsible for theft (see Chapter 8, Patterns That Could Indicate Theft.)

Assuming there was an employee named, it is not necessary that the entire claim be completed or paid before contact with the employee is made. The reason for the contact is to obtain the employee's version of the allegations, and if there is no question on the fact of theft, try and determine how the theft was done, and if there were any other employees or non-employees that assisted in the theft.

It is most important to obtain information on the amount stolen by the employee and if that amount matches what the employer believes was stolen. Employees do not keep records of the amounts they have stolen. Over the years I found what I call my unofficial 1/3 rule. If an employee admitted to the theft of $5,000 he probably stole $15,000. It seemed that I had a number of cases where the employees admitted to about 1/3 of the amounts that were finally agreed to with the insureds. These settlements were based on loss documentation, not on what the employees said they stole.

The better the documentation of the employer's loss, the better the chances of obtaining full cooperation from the employee to include the employee signing any confession and agreeing to some sort of **"restitution."** This can be important during the subrogation and recovery phase of the loss. Unless the employee has accurate records, the documentation of the employer would carry more weight than the employee simply stating"I did not think I stole so much."

Once any coverage questions have been eliminated and the loss documentation agreed to, the company representative will have the employer complete a **"subrogation receipt"** for the amount of the **"covered loss"**, minus any policy deductible and credits from the employee's pay, retirement plan or voluntary payments. You should check with your CPA or attorney for guidance as to what credits you can accept or take from the employee prior to a criminal conviction.

You will note I highlighted the words "covered loss". What I was referring to were the situations where either the loss amount was a compromise between the insurance company and the insured, or where the insured's loss exceeds the policy limit. The bonding company cannot be responsible for paying anymore than the policy limit and because of that, they can only have the insured sign a subrogation receipt for that amount, minus any deductible.

You, the insured could still have a portion of the loss that is not payable by the insurance company open for direct recovery by you from the employee. This brings up two concerns: one is whether you and the insurance company should determine the total loss even if it exceeds policy limits, and the second is where do you, the insured, stand in line of those who are to be paid back for a loss. The first concern will be discussed here, the second will be discussed in the next chapter.

When the amount of coverage is substantial, there is never a concern about spending time and expense in determining how much of the loss to prove or document. However, when you have an insured that carries a small limit, say $10,000, and the information from the records, after "discovery" seems to indicate that the loss may be larger than the policy limit, and perhaps requiring a lot of time and paperwork to prove, a decision has to be made on how much of the loss over the limit should be verified.

CASE HISTORY: A loss I am currently working on involves what appears to be a theft of money from the cash register of a store owned by this corporation. The insured carries only $10,000 of employee dishonesty coverage. However, from the information I have reviewed, which was compiled by the company accountant, the loss could have been going on for over a year, and could be over $40,000. After doing a review of only two months sales, the loss amounts in that time limit exceed the policy limit. Thus, once the insured completes the proof of loss, payment up to the policy limit should be made. Since the insured has not as yet completed the Fidelity Proof of Loss, I have not tried to interview any of the employees that worked in the store. From what I have been told, the employees most likely responsible for the theft are not going to cooperate. Therefore, it does not appear that I will have any confession to assist in determining the size of the loss.

What if the loss is larger than the policy limit? The insured would like to recover what they can. Who is responsible for determining the total amount of the loss? Should the bonding company incur the expense of an investigator like myself, or the hiring of an auditor to verify the loss the company will not have to pay for? Should the insurer tell the insured it is his responsibility to verify the loss, at his expense.

Instructions from the insurance companies can vary, determined by several factors. What is the potential total loss, how difficult is it to verify, and what is the amount of that loss in relation to the amount of coverage. It is basically an insurance company decision, based on the policy wording of that insurance company's policy. The standard order is that the insurance company is not reimbursed for what it paid, until the insured is paid for loss above the policy limit. I will discuss this in the next chapter.

You, the insured also have to decide whether you wish to incur the accounting cost to verify an additional amount of loss, which both exceeds the policy limit, and incurs additional expense that you may never recover. (See Restitution in the following chapter.)

Two things are certain: the employer cannot expect the bonding company to pay for the expense in proving that part of a loss that is more than the coverage, and a civil or criminal court is not going to award compensation or restitution if any amount claimed by the insured is not documented.

Up to this point the writings in the book have been for the benefit of those who carry or need employee dishonesty coverage, or those who work with or for employers, or companies that have a professional relationship with those employers, or bonding companies. However, there is a large group in the corporate world that can benefit from many chapters in this book, especially from this point on. I am referring to those large corporations that carry high retention (read deductibles) on their employee theft coverage. These are companies that can afford to self insure a $100,000 or larger employee theft loss. These companies have **"Risk Managers"** that are supposed to know how to handle these losses, as well as worker's compensation and any other self insured risk exposure.

As to how the larger retention affects the insured, the insurance company does not become involved until the amount of loss reaches the retention limit. Some insurance companies require the insured to send a copy of the loss notice to the insurance carrier, who simply files it away, or perhaps makes occasional calls to check on the status of the loss. This continues until the loss is concluded or the amount of loss is going to exceed the retention limit.

The investigation of the loss, by the corporation, is usually done by an in house investigator, or a Third Party Administrator, (an outside contractor that investigates losses under a contract price), or by the use of a Private Investigator or Certified Protection Professional.

Once an employee theft loss reaches the **"retention"** level, the insurance carrier will probably hire a CPA to verify the loss documentation. After the loss is concluded, the claim enters the "Subrogation, Recovery and Restitution" phase.

Before moving on to the next chapter you should have some understanding of what is termed in the bond policy as **"Valuation of settlement"**. This is the wording that spells out what values the insurance companies place on the different areas of loss that can be sustained by the insured in an employee theft claim. There are three categories of loss that can be sustained by an employer as result of employee theft. They are: money, securities and property. Each will be discussed so you have a good understanding of what you can expect should a loss involve one or more of these areas.

MONEY:

- Face value of currency or coin, bank notes, traveler's or certified checks, money orders held for sale to the public.
- The amount that checks are written for from the checking account of the employer and deposited into the account of the employee.
- The amount listed on fraudulent vouchers or invoices and paid by or from the employer's accounts payable account.

Money is paid out at those values. There is no consideration for loss of interest or loss of use of any money stolen by the employee. In other words if a theft took place over several years before it was discovered and the loss (face amount) was $200,000, the most the bonding company would pay is the $200,000. There would be no payment to the insured for the interest the insured's company could have made on that money.

This loss of interest **is** a loss to the employer and should be added as part of the employer's claim against those responsible for the loss. This will be discussed further in Chapter 8, Subrogation, Recovery and Restitution. You should speak with your CPA or attorney for guidance here. As you will see from the example below, in a large loss the loss of use of that money, over time, can be substantial. Using the example of a $200,000 loss stolen over eight years, which, for the sake of simplicity was stolen at the rate $25,000 a year, the loss of interest (at 5%) would be over $50,000. Here is how that works out.

year 1.	employee steals	$25,000.00
	5% interest	1,250.00
	total first year	26,250.00
year 2.	employee steals add.	25,000.00
	total Prin.& Interest	51,250.00
	5% int.	2,562.50
	total second year	53,812.50
year 3.	employee steals add.	25,000.00
	total P & I.	78,812.50
	5% int.	3,940.63
	total third year	82,753.13
year 4.	employee steals add.	25,000.00
	total P & I.	107,753.13
	5% int.	5,387.66
	total fourth year	113,140.79
year 5.	employee steals add.	25,000.00
	total P & I.	138,140.79
	5% int.	6,907.04
	total fifth year	145,047.83

year 6.	employee steals add.	25,000.00
	total P & I.	170,047.83
	5% int.	8,502.39
	total sixth year	178,550.22

year 7.	employee steals add.	25,000.00
	total P & I.	203,550.22
	5% int.	10,177.51
	total seventh year	213,727.73

year 8.	employee steals add.	25,000.00
	total P & I.	238,727.73
	5% int.	11,936.39
	total in eight years	$250,664.12
	deduct principle lost	−200,000.00
	simple interest lost	50,664.12

As you can see this is a lot of money. On smaller losses, or a theft that does not last as long as this example did, the loss of use of money and interest on that money is less, and it may not be worthwhile trying to add that loss of interest to your claim.

The bonding companies can pay, at their option, money issued by other countries. That of course would only occur if money from another country was stolen. Again **"Face Value"** is used here.

If the employer lost money from another country but wants to be paid in U.S. dollars, the rate of exchange between the two currencies that existed on the day the loss was discovered will be used for that determination of "face Value".

SECURITIES:

The second category is loss of **"Securities"**. The CRIME GENERAL PROVISIONS form list "Securities" as:

1. Negotiable and non negotiable instruments or contracts representing either "money" or other property and includes.

a. Tokens, tickets, revenue and other stamps or the unused value in a postage meter in current use.

b. Evidences of debt issued in connection with credit or charge cards, which are issued by you.

The loss of "securities" will be determined by their value at the close of the business day on the day the loss was discovered. The insurance company has several options as to the payment of these stolen securities. They may pay the value of the security or replace them in kind. If that is done the employer (you) must assign all rights of ownership and interest of those securities to the insurance (bonding) company.

PROPERTY:

The final category consists of property that has been stolen or damaged by the employee and was either owned by the employer, held by the employer, or that the employer was legally liable for. This property could be either equipment or vehicles owned or used by the employer or inventory owned by said employer.

The important point here is that the value used, is the **"Actual Cash Value"** of that property on the day the loss was discovered. In the insurance language "actual cash value" is referred to as **"ACV"**. This is determined by taking the cost to replace the item, and deducting depreciation. The difference is the "ACV".

The maximum amount that can be paid for any or all of these categories cannot exceed the amount of bond coverage issued to the employer.

DENIAL OF CLAIM:

Before moving to the next chapter, some reference to denial of claim should be made. If the insurance company feels that the documentation submitted does not represent a covered loss under the bond, or if there are exclusions that appear to void coverage, they may deny your claim. If that occurs, contact your insurance agent as soon as you are notified of the denial by the insurance company representative. Your agent would first ask the insurance company representative to explain the reason for the denial. If you and the agent are not satisfied with that explanation, your agent may submit a report of the loss, and denial to the Office of the Insurance Commissioner in your state for a review. If the denial stands, your final recourse would be to sue the insurance company. Legal costs involved in any of these reviews, appeals or trials are not covered by the policy.

Another circumstance that can sometimes preceed a "denial of claim" occurs when the insured submits improper or incomplete documentation either on the "fidelity proof of loss" form or in loss information submitted with the "proof." When that occurs the insurance company may **"reject the proof".** This means that the insurance company will return the "proof" that had been submitted, and require that the insured supply new or more complete information before the insurance company will consider the loss any further.

The adjustment of any loss is important because it represents where the insured is reimbursed by the insurance company for the agreed covered loss. This settlement opens the next phase of the claim where it is usually the insurance company, that looks for reimbursement. This is covered in the next chapter, "Subrogation, Recovery and Restitution".

Chapter Seven

Subrogation, Recovery, Restitution

After the adjustment process has been completed, the insurance company will need to have a **"Subrogation Receipt" (appendix 4)** signed by an officer of the insured, for the amount the insurance company has paid. This document allows the insurance company to recover from the employee, or anyone else found legally responsible for the theft. This would apply to any type of insured loss, but any discussion here is focused on employee theft.

For example, say the agreed loss was $160,000. The insured carried a deductible of $10,000. If the insurance company paid to their insured $150,000 the insurance company would be **"subrogated"** for that amount.

In the case of a self insured with a retention of $100,000 and a $160,000 loss, the company would have a subrogation receipt signed for $60,000. The term **"legally responsible"** would normally apply to the employee that either confessed to the theft, or was found guilty in criminal court or liable in civil court for that theft. However, the responsible party could also be a non-employee that worked with the employee in carrying out the theft. It could also refer to the company hired by the insured to do the accounting or auditing of the company's financials, if it can be proven that the accountants or auditors erred in not recognizing and reporting **blatant** indications of fraud and theft. Or the insurance company may try to subrogate against another insurance company's insured, if that insured's actions, perhaps poor hiring practices, allowed you to hire someone that you would otherwise have never hired. Employment agencies are the obvious group here.

There are many other possibilities, the important point is the amount of loss paid by your insurance company, allows them and only them, to try and recover from whomever they are able, the amount paid to you.

RECOVERY:

Following right behind subrogation is **Recovery**. This is the amount that both the insured and the bonding company hope to get back from what was lost and or paid under the adjustment of the loss. The main player in this recovery is the insurance company, since they are usually the entity that has paid the most of any loss, and has the right to "recovery" of what they paid out. But recovery is also important to the insured or employer, for two reasons. The first reason is whatever has been paid to the insured from the bonding company goes against the insured's loss experience. This could have an effect on whether the insured is **renewed** for the next policy period or perhaps there could be a premium rate increase. If the insurance company collects what was paid, the only expense that the company would have is the cost of the investigation, accounting or legal fees paid in the adjustment or subrogation phase of the loss. The second reason could be the deductible or "retention" that the insured had to pay before they received the net claim amount from the insurance company. (You must check with your insurance agent concerning deductibles. Many of my insurance clients have historically offered employee theft coverage with very small deductibles. It was not unusual for a large $200 million corporation to have no deductible for employee theft coverage and that was with a $500,000 limit. However, I have received some information that this may be changing).

If the deductible was small, say $1,000 that may not be a great loss to the insured, but if the deductible or retention is in five figures or higher, then that is an amount you would want to return to the cash flow of the company.

Your own policy wording may vary, depending on the carrier and type policy in force, but normally the recovery order is as follows:

1. Any amount that the insured has proven and sustained, and is above the limit of insurance, and the insured's deductible, is paid first.
2. Next, is the bonding company. They are paid up to the amount that they paid to their insured.
3. Finally, the insured is reimbursed their deductible.

In a loss where the amount stolen was significantly more than the coverage, it is very important for the insured to do whatever is possible to recover the amount they lost. Added to this amount is the claim for loss of use of that money. Referring back to the last chapter with the example of the $200,000 loss over eight years that turned into an additional loss of interest of over $50,000, the insured has a right to claim that interest as part of their loss.

In my opinion that interest becomes part of the loss that is not paid under the bond, and should be considered under number 1. (above) as an amount that should be paid to the insured before the bonding company is paid. Of course the amount of lost interest, as with any other part of the loss that is not recoverable under the bond must be proven or sustained. The expense to prove that "additional loss" must be borne by the insured.

The amount that the insured is trying to collect is known as "compensatory loss". In some states the insured could also claim a loss of "punitive damages". Here you must refer to your attorney for instruction.

Here is an example of where I believe an insured should be entitled to collect, from the employee, more than what the face amount of loss was. I should note, this loss was not investigated by me. The information is somewhat vague, meaning I did not ask for names, dates, or locations. The loss information was presented to me at one of my seminars. The brief facts are that a well liked employee of a company was successful in embezzling $500,000 from the employer over several years time. When the loss was discovered, the employee admitted to the theft and supposedly stated that he would pay back the $500,000 he stole if the company would not prosecute.

The company agreed to accept the money as a full and final settlement, and did not prosecute. Sometime later the company officials were informed that the employee had taken the money he had stolen and invested wisely. He allegedly turned the money into an additional 1.2 million dollars. With the invested money the employee was supposedly able to retire.

Whether or not this story is true is not important. The point here is that someone who steals from your company, who has caused untold difficulties with personnel, including loss of time by the managers in proving the loss, and of course the effect the loss of money had on the company itself, has no business profiting from his illegal deeds.

My recommendation to any employer that has sustained a significant loss, is to show no mercy on the employee that stole from them, and to try and collect all they can from whomever they can.

Here is a short list of entities that you as the employer or the insurance company may go after to recover what was stolen.

1. Employee- Obviously, this is the most likely person to try and recover from, since he or she stole from you. Unfortunately, this person may be the least likely to have any funds readily available to pay back what was stolen. There are several reasons for this. If the person stole to support a habit such as drugs or gambling, historically whatever they stole has been used to buy new drugs or pay old debts. If they kicked their habit, or hit a big winner gambling they probably would not have continued the theft. This is seldom the case however.

   If the person stole for greed, they usually do not save the money, but use it to buy more personal possessions. Even in a case where the money was used to pay for uninsured medical treatment, usually what was stolen went for that purpose.

   Here are a few places to look for reimbursement from the employee:.

   a. Unpaid salary- This should be a voluntary payment made by the employee who has confessed to the theft. Never try taking this money if the identity of the employee is not clear. Also, I do not recommend taking possession of this without written permission from the employee and/or his or her attorney.
   b. Retirement/ 401K plans- Depending on the type plan, getting money out before retirement age of the employee may create severe tax penalties. This area has to be researched by your company attorney or pension consultant.

    c. Personal assets- Whether you are able to attach or take personal assets will depend on what that asset is and the facts of the theft. The employee's home is the place that may have the largest value, but it is the most difficult to attach.

CASE HISTORY: *In a large hospital loss involving over $200,000 stolen over nine years, the employee stole to pay off large credit card debt as well as help in the down payment on a home. The spouse was not a large wage earner working only part time and making less than $5,000 per year. There was nothing in the investigation to indicate that the spouse knew that the theft was taking place. Unless something in the additional investigation by the bonding company turns up new information, the employee acted on his own. The home they bought is titled as "Tenants by the Entirety" which is the most common way husbands and wives title their joint property. Current law does not allow the employer or the bonding company to attach the home, when titled like this, unless it can be proven that the spouse knew about the theft and continued to enjoy the monetary results of that theft. This rule does not apply to other real estate title arrangements.*

There is sometimes equity in the home which can be used to pay off the debt. I will discuss this in **"Restitution"**.

    d. Other assets are fair game. They could be securities, boats vehicles, and money in bank accounts.

  2. Non-employees- In cases where a friend or relative of the employee helps in the theft, the friend becomes a party to criminal activity, and can have assets similar to the employee's attached.

  3. Accountants/ auditors- this category has to be separated into several groups. First, I shall discuss the accountant or bookkeeper firm you hire to review your bank statement, in-

voices or vouchers on a monthly or quarterly basis. If you have an employee stealing through one of the areas that the accountant is balancing, depending on the exact method of theft, and the work that accountant has been hired to do, it may result in a claim under the **"Errs and Omissions of the Accountant"** if they failed to uncover something they should have. I will give you an easy example, In Chapter 10 I write about methods of theft involving checkbooks. One case history that I write about is the office manager for two doctors that stole $40,000 in several months. She simply wrote checks to herself and when the bank statement came in the mail, she removed the real cancelled checks and replaced them with copies from the copy machine showing a vendor that matched the check stub in the check book. The doctors did not have monthly balancing of their checkbook by an accountant. But if they did, as you will read in the detailed account I would think any accountant would have seen something wrong and reported it. If they did not then I think an"Errs and Omissions" loss would have taken place. Every case has to be looked at closely.

The next group of accountants is the **"year end auditor"**. Normally you engage an outside accounting firm to conduct your end of year audit of your corporation. The first step is the **"Engagement Letter"** which summarizes what the accounting firm is being hired to do. They should follow standard <u>GENERAL ACCEPTED ACCOUNTING PRINCIPLES</u> (GAAP) in this audit.

I want to state here, that it is not the intent of this book to go into a detailed study of what does and does not indicate that you as the employer and retainer of an outside auditing firm, have a right of recovery from the work submitted by that auditor. My only purpose is to make sure you have a better understanding of what the outside auditor's responsibilities are, and for you to know that there are possibilities of recovery if those responsibilities are not met.

When fraud (employee theft) is discovered by other means than from the audit, everyone looks to the auditor and says something like"why didn't he find this." The next thought, is to consider placing the "Errs and Omissions" carrier of the auditor on notice. Before that is done, you should have a detailed discussion with your corporate attorney, in house controller or CFO, and possibly with another accounting firm. The reason for that discussion is to obtain a professional determination as to whether the auditor overlooked something in the audit that should have been noticed by the auditor and reported to management for further investigation.

A review of the engagement letter should be done along with the report that the auditor may have sent the company from any previous as well as current audits. These **"Management Letters"** summarize what the auditor suggests as a result of the audit. The letter may go into several aspects of the financial operation of the company, to include comments about **"Internal Controls"**. If past "management letters" have suggested changes in the internal controls and those changes were not made, then the auditor more than likely is not professionally responsible for any employee theft that arose because those controls were not checked.

Another determination is whether the auditor used "GAAP" guidelines in that audit. You will have to rely on someone with an accounting background to help you with that question.

One of the key words in the auditor's work is whether the item being audited is **"material"** to the operation of the company and in turn "material" to the financial statements. An item may be considered "material" if it represents a certain percentage of the overall income to the company. If the item falls below that percentage, then the auditor is not required to **"test or prove"** the documents that may or may not back up that item.

In chapter 10 I write about the in house accountant that knew the material level of the "reimbursement to patient account" was over $70,000 every fiscal year. She stole no more than $70,000 every year. When the hospital had their outside auditors audit the financials of the corporation they did not find this theft. The reason, the theft was too low in comparison to the overall income of the hospital, thus there was no requirement to check or prove any of the disbursements in that department.

As I will discuss beginning with chapter 9, "Management Controls" are the responsibility and function of management. This means that the management or owners of a business or corporation are responsible for setting in place controls that will hopefully deter, stop or discover fraud.

Up to this fiscal year, auditors were only required to fulfill what was written in the "engagement letters", using proper procedures. If they thought there could be a problem they would tell management about it in the "management letters". Auditors may not also be trained in **"Forensic Accounting"**, that area of accounting that looks for and discovers fraud. So unless there was a "material misstatement" or some blatant indication of fraud, you could not expect the auditor to find fraud for you. That may change after December 15, 1997. According to the **AICPA (American Institute of Certified Public Accountants)** the auditors responsibilities in doing audits will change . In AICPA Professional Standards, section AU316.01 states in part **"The auditor has a responsibility to plan and perform the audit to obtain reasonable assurance about whether the financial statements are free of material misstatement, whether caused by error or fraud."** The information goes on, in technical terms laying out guidance for the auditors. My interpretation is that the auditors will still follow the outline of work as stated in the "engagement letter", but that the auditor will be asking for more documents and backup as compared to the past. I have known a number of CPA's from years in the investigation of employee theft. All seemed very competent during those audits we were involved with. From my experience with them, they are not going to place their names on an audit, with these new guidelines, without looking for and getting every document necessary to explain all transactions that might be considered **material to the financial statement.** The end result will be a more detailed audit, and as a result one that is more expensive.

However, in turn, the legal responsibility for the auditor will increase. These new requirements on the auditors will place tremendous importance on the "engagement letter". As the employer you want to make sure the letter spells out exactly how you want your audit conducted.

4. Banks and other savings institutions-The areas where banks become vulnerable to claims of recovery from employee theft revolve around the checking account of the company, and improper deposits of corporate business into personal accounts.

As you are probably aware, when a company opens a checking account, the bank chosen for that business requires several documents signed by corporate officers. One is a corporate resolution which confirms the existence of the company, and lists several key officers of that company. Along with this is a bank signature card that will list the names and signatures of those officers or company officials authorized to write checks for the company. This card will also list the number of signatures for those checks.

Bank culpability can occur in two areas. The first is when the bank tellers do not check to make sure the signatures on the checks are consistent with the signatures on the signature card. If an employee is using an unauthorized name on the check, or if the signature does not resemble the signature of one of the officers selected to write on the account, the bank may be responsible for any amount stolen using this method. However, the bank's legal responsibility decreases as time goes on. At the present time the bank's liability for allowing an improper signature to go through, is one year from the date of that transaction.

The banking laws have different time limits in which a complaint can be filed, depending on what the transaction is. It has been explained to me that if there is a problem with the balance in your account you have thirty days from the last statement to claim any errors. If you claim a forged maker of your check, you have one year to file the claim. If it is a forged endorsement you have three years. I suggest you check with your attorney for guidance in your state. Additionally, I feel that there will be more changes in the future because many banks are not returning cancelled checks on large business accounts. This procedure will make it more difficult to spot misuse of checks.

The second area of bank negligence occurs when the bank allows the deposit of a check with a business name payee to be deposited into a personal account.

CASE HISTORY: *In this case the employee was a salesman for a computer consulting company. He was in need of money, so he began depositing checks that were made payable to his employer, into his own personal account. He would contact the client and ask that he be able to pick up the checks for payment* *of services. He would pick up the check and take it to his bank for deposit into his own personal account.*

In reviewing some of the checks involved, all were made payable to the company, for services or consulting fees. The banking code requires these type of checks to be deposited only into a business account. As you will read the bank employees were negligent.

RESTITUTION:

This is defined in Black's Law Dictionary as "The act of restoring; restoration; restoration of anything to its rightful owner; the act of making good or giving equivalent for any loss, damage or injury." The definition continues "A person who has been unjustly enriched at the expense of another is required to make restitution."

There is no doubt that when employee theft has been proven, and the loss can be attributed to a specific employee or employees (more than one being responsible not simply a group from which one or more are **thought** to be responsible), reimbursement or restitution is in order.

As I had written earlier in this chapter, the amount to be paid can be to both the employer and the insurance company. The amount to be reimbursed and to the whom depends on the amount and extent of the proven loss, what was paid by the bonding company, as well as the retention and or deductible that were in effect.

With the previous text on "subrogation" and the "order of recovery" considered in any restitution situation, the following restitution information can, for the most part apply to either the employer or the bonding company.

The most likely place to look for recovery/restitution is the employee. If the money stolen is no longer available, the employee's assets, with some limitations can be reached. The largest asset may be the employee's home. Granted you may not be able to force a sale of the home due to the way the home is titled, but the employee may be willing to borrow from any equity in the home to pay off the amount stolen.

The employee may have savings, securities or other tangible assets that the employee may be willing to sell in order to pay off the amount stolen. Normally this is not the case, but there are exceptions.

The one other area which I have found to be a source of restitution, is money from relatives of the employee. Sometimes the employee will approach relatives and ask for monetary assistance, even though the employee may not explain the real reason for the loan. This is something between the employee and his or her relatives. The employer or the insurance company should never make any contact with the relatives of the employee. All you should do is provide ideas to the employee for sources of money for the restitution.

CIVIL AND CRIMINAL COURT:

You may be thinking what can the employer or the subrogation department of the bonding company do to force the employee to repay what was taken. What "leverage"' do you have? In most cases the employee will have lost his job from the employer he stole from. The employee may not have the assets to make payment to the employer or bonding company, without burdening himself and possibly his family with more financial obligations. There may be hard feelings from things that were said by the employer of or to the employee during the investigation of the loss. The "leverage" is criminal or civil litigation. Under current law, the employer is the true **"victim"** in this type of theft. Only the victim can pursue recovery in either the civil or criminal courts. I have written earlier that I am in favor of the employer notifying the authorities whenever there is an employee theft loss of over $5,000. However when the loss is discovered you may not know what the extent of loss is. But there is time before any decision concerning the authorities has to, if at all, be made.

I have experienced the full gamut of reactions from employers concerning whether to begin a criminal process against the employee. Some are so angry with what the employee has done, they want that employee punished and do not care what it costs the employer or the state to prosecute. Other employers are reluctant to notify the police because they do not want the publicity, or they do not want to jeopardize working things out with the employee directly. Recently a manager of a large dealership explained the reasons he did not want to bring in the police:

- He did not want to have to spend more time explaining and proving his claim to the States Attorney, losing more time from work,
- Time away from business testifying in court,
- Possibly incurring further physical repercussions from the employee.

These are all valid reasons and concerns. This is a decision that should be discussed with your legal and insurance advisers. **Remember, do what is best for your practice, business or corporation. Do not make a decision based on any sympathy for the employee.** The employee certainly does not care about you or your company, if he did he would not have stolen from you. Every case is different and decisions should be made according to the facts, cooperation and chance of restitution without police and the States Attorney involved.

I must state, however, from my years of experience in this field, the best way to insure that you will get cooperation from the employee is to use the possibility of criminal prosecution as an avenue to obtain recovery. When the employee realizes that if he is convicted of this crime he is looking at several years probation as a first time offender, and perhaps jail time if he is a repeat offender, the employee will usually cooperate. From what I have seen or been told by those that have been prosecuted, at least in Maryland, there is little chance of jail for a first timer. The trial judge however, will usually attach probation to restitution. This means that the judge may place the employee/defendant on five years probation (for example) as long as that employee pays to the state a certain amount towards paying back what was stolen. The defendant pays the state, and the state forwards those payments, in the form of state checks to the employer or the bonding company.

If the employee fails to make those payments, or is found guilty of another felony, the judge may revoke the five year probation, and the defendant will start serving time in jail. The defendant will still have that debt to repay upon his completion of the jail term.

Under current wording in the majority of bond polices, there is no requirement that an employer/insured notify the police when there is an employee theft loss. In some states there may be a requirement that you, as the employer, must notify the police whenever there is a felony, which employee theft usually is. You should check with the States Attorney's Office in your area, or your corporate attorney for assistance.

The other area of litigation is through the civil courts. This action can be brought by the employer or the insurance company. There are several major differences between the two court systems. In the criminal court the state or county prosecutes the theft and there is no cost to you for legal fees. However, in a civil trial you or the insurance company will have to engage your own attorney for trial. Unless the attorney was to take the case on a percent of recovery, the professional charges of your attorney are not part of your loss, and cannot be recovered from the employee. (Nor is there any recovery to you the employer, by the insurance company for those fees.)

An additional difference is that there is no probation or jail time in a civil suit. If the employee is found responsible for the theft, the judge or jury will award damages, and can either allow the attachment of property and other assets, and/or garnishment of wages. The order can also force the sale of assets to pay the debt. **Garnishment** of wages is the county, city or state's method of requiring the employee's future employer to set aside a certain amount money from the defendant's pay, in order to reimburse a past debt. The garnishment order will not indicate to the new employer the reason for the garnishment.

VOLUNTARY SETTLEMENT BY THE "EMPLOYEE":

Should the employee decide that he or she wishes to settle the loss with the employer or the bonding company, there are in essence two different settlement options. The first is a full and final settlement of the entire amount that you and the employee agree was taken. This would be for 100 percent of the agreed amount to be paid at one time. From my experience, full payments for large losses seldom occur because the money is just not available.

The second settlement, and the one that seems to occur more frequently would be payment over a period of time. The amount could be for the full amount of loss, plus whatever other charges and expenses the employer or bonding company can try to add to the loss amount. Settlement could also be a compromised figure. The reason for the compromise may be that the employer cannot prove all the loss amount that they claim was taken by the employee, or the employer or bonding company would rather take a percent of the loss up front than wait for a trial date and years of the employee paying off the loss. Here is an example why.

CASE HISTORY: I had a $5,000 loss from a seafood restaurant in Baltimore. After my investigation, the seafood restaurant employer was paid. The employee was arrested, convicted and given five years probation, tied to restitution. The state did not place a minimum amount to be paid. For some reason the state put my company name on the checks along with the name of the bonding company. For the next three years (usually every quarter) my company would receive checks from the state for $15.00, $25.00. or $35.00 amounts. I would endorse the checks, and mail them to the bonding company, along with a short cover letter. Although I did not total the man hours on my part and the part of the bonding company in processing these checks, I am sure the cost in man hours, was over $5,000.

In the above example there was no opportunity to ask for or receive any settlement for less than the amount of loss. The employee was not cooperative with the employer or myself. I am sure that if the employer had not prosecuted, I doubt the bonding company would have gotten any money because the employee had no assets. This way the state **requires the payment or else it is jail for the employee**. And, as I have written, based from my experiences, garnishment of wages does not bother some defalcators, but the prospect of jail if they do not continue to pay does get their attention.

There can be several legal documents drawn up to properly complete any settlement arrangement. Your company attorney is best suited for preparing this document. If the bonding company is involved the document used is referred to as a **"Promissory Note."** This document states the total amount that is to be paid, and the interest for any amount that is not paid up front. For example, in a $20,000 loss with that amount agreed to, the bonding company would normally not accept a promissory note unless several thousand dollars were put down at the time the note was to be signed. They could request up to 1/3 of the amount. They would then accept a note for the remainder, to be paid monthly over the next five years with the unpaid balance paid at a low to moderate interest rate. For this type of payment the employer or bonding company agrees not to attach any property or begin any civil litigation. If however, the employee fails to keep up with the payments, the note is void and all remaining amounts are due or litigation will begin. Some notes will include the right to ask for attorney's fees and other court cost in the litigation.

BANKRUPTCY:

This would be filed by the employee as a way to get out of paying the amount owed to you or the bonding company. In the years that I have investigated employee theft losses, only in two cases were there any indications that the defalcators wanted to file bankruptcy as a way to avoid paying back what they had stolen. In both cases there had been convictions in criminal court and I understand that the amounts awarded in restitution could not be **"discharged"** by filing bankruptcy.

I have reviewed the USCS code that discusses bankruptcy and I found the writing confusing. There seemed to be examples where a debt from a fraud or embezzlement could not be discharged by filing bankruptcy and there were examples that indicated they could be free of that debt if they filed.

I have been advised that there are motions that can filed with the court by your attorney to prevent any bankruptcy filed be the embezzler discharging the amount owed as a result of a theft.

Since the discovery of employee theft results in additional financial and employment problems for the **"defalcator"** one may wonder why do employees steal. Chapter 8 will discuss some of the reasons.

Chapter Eight

Patterns That Could Indicate Theft

Who Steals and Why They Steal

Quite often insurance agents who have employers as clients, as well as the employers themselves, have asked me what are signs that an employee is stealing, or may be inclined to steal in the future. I have also been asked, what kind of employee steals and why.

PATTERNS:

Although all employers want to have hard working, dedicated employees, these are the same behaviors that could apply to dishonest employees. I am not referring to the employee who has a drug addiction, misses days from work and when he returns, needs to steal inventory to support his habit. These type employees can indeed cause considerable monetary problems for their employer, but these thefts normally do not last a long time. And because they do not last years, the loss may be smaller and not as financially damaging to the company as other loses.

When I refer to an employee that is a thief and is also hard working, it is because that employee has to work very hard to keep up his scheme, as well as do his regular work, so no one will notice anything wrong with his work production. If he is not at work, or not working the job that has been given to him, he runs the risk of losing that job, which will cause him to lose his source of secondary income.

The majority of employees who work for their company put in long hours and are honest people who want to help the company do well. By working hard they believe that the company will prosper noy. the employee will benefit in the future as well. You as the employer have the responsibility to recognize and reward those employees. By reading this chapter, you, the employer, should be able to recognize patterns or signs of where this hard work and dedication for the company stop, and possible theft or other problems that could lead to theft begins.

These patterns, or actions by the employee, should be looked at closely when the employee also has a responsible position with access to the company cash (including deposits and investments), accounts payable (AP), invoices, computer system, cash register (if a retail establishment or business), or inventory. (I call these the **"CYA" departments, which stand for "Control Your Assets).**

One of the patterns that I have seen is the employee that comes to work early or stays late at night. Everyone knows that anyone in sales, production or management can be expected to work late once in awhile in order to prepare a presentation or complete a project for a client. But when this pattern of work occurs frequently, and you, as the employer, cannot place a specific reason for these extra hours, there could be a problem.

I have investigated several large losses where the employee would come to work early or stay late, so she could carry out her embezzlement while other employees or supervisors were not there.

CASE HISTORY: I just completed an investigation with a large health care corporation where their accounting manager stole several hundred thousand dollars from their "AP" department. The manager would come in early, before anyone else, and pull the first two "AP" checks off of the continuous feed on the printer that printed the checks. The two checks were always blank. The manager would type his own name on the checks as payee, sign the checks using a signature stamp, and deposit them into his account. This manager could not have found time to do this during the regular work day. He was too busy and his staff would wonder why he was going into the check writing room. (A complete summary of this theft will be discussed in Chapter 10).

If an employee is using a company computer to generate false invoices or inventory, he or she has to do this before their regular computer work starts. There is normally too much work during the regular work hours for someone in this position to find time to carry out this type of theft. It has and can be done, but it is more difficult. Success would depend on where the employee work station is in relation to other employees. Certainly, if the employee has his own office, it is easier to carry on the scheme during the work day.

Another pattern I found during my investigations is where the employee does not want to take a vacation. This may seem odd, but if an employee is running a theft where he is using the company checkbook and or accounts payable along with the bank statement, she is afraid to take time off from work. The reason for this behavior, is she does not know who may be asked to write a check while she is away. If she is writing checks to herself, the substitute clerk or bookkeeper may see something in the checkbook that will lead to a discovery of the theft. The thief also wants to be there when the bank statement arrives in the mail because she wants to remove any checks that were written to herself. (In a larger company, the banks may only send the check numbers back, which is easier for the thief, but she still needs to hide the amounts of those checks). As an employer, you want to make sure all employees take vacations, especially those in sensitive areas. An employee that refuses a vacation should be watched carefully.

An additional pattern or sign comes under the word **"appearance"**. This can be the most difficult gauge as a sign of possible problems that could involve employee dishonesty. When I refer to appearance, you probably think I am referring to a style of dress or how the employee keeps his or her personal look, such as clothing, hair, make up if a woman, or facial hair if a man. Granted someone that has a severe addiction could have an unkept look about them as I will discuss later. What I am referring to is how the employee works with other employees, what you hear of his or her life style from those employees, and what you observe in jewelry or clothing the employee wears, places he or she goes or cars the employee drives. These observations **may** indicate that an employee is living beyond what his or her salary would buy.

What makes this so difficult is that although you know the income of your employee, you do not know what the income may be from the employee's spouse or "significant other" should the employee be living with someone and sharing expenses. With the advent of the two income household, buying power is increased, and with the "buy now, pay later"philosophy of stores, and the low lease rates on vehicles, one can portray a life style that might be over what his or her income would seem to support. Therefore, as the old expression goes, appearances can be deceiving.

However, if you feel that these "appearances" present something more than what the total income should buy, and the employee is in a "CYA" position, some investigation is in order.

An investigation is also suggested if you have an employee whose personal appearance has deteriorated or his interaction with other employees has changed. These could be as a result of legitimate personal or family stress that is manifesting itself in this manner. It could also be a warning sign that your employee has an addiction or financial need that requires more money than his income provides.

CASE HISTORY: An auto dealer had a supervisor of new and used car accessories and parts steal over $15,000 in four months. During the course of my investigation, the insured described the employee's physical appearance as pale and drawn looking. He frequently had an unkept look about him. He acted like he had a cold for a long time. He also missed time from work. During this time management received word from vendors that they were not being paid for the accessories sent to the supervisor for installation on the cars and trucks. This should have been a red flag to management. Instead of conducting an investigation such as checking invoices against sales records or place someone else in the office to work with the supervisor, they spoke to the "employee". He said he was behind in the paper work but that he would take care of it. More losses took place before the loss was finally discovered. Because of the actions by the dealership, the new losses were not covered under the bond policy. During the verbal confession given by the "employee", he admitted to a drug problem.

As the employer, you are not going to see the results of theft immediately. One of my larger loss investigations involved theft that lasted over a nine year period of time. Even if you have noticed that there is a possible problem, you may choose to ignore it, thinking that "they would never steal from me". You have to realize that **the person you hired ten years ago, may not be the same person today.** There could be personal or family life style changes that make them a candidate for employee dishonesty. You have to periodically re-evaluate all employees that are in the "CYA" areas I referred to before. Obviously, if you are running a medium size corporation that has a personnel or human resources department, you have to educate those managers on what to look for, because if you don't, they won't.

WHO'S A THIEF AND WHY:

This brings me to the section of who are the employees that steal, and why. I must first state that these comments are based on over two decades of investigation into this field, as well as what has been given to me from insurance, legal and accounting professionals. What is being written here is an answer to many of those that have asked these questions to me. However, I am not going to try and provide you the reader, with any sort of psychological profile of a thief. Nor will I provide any conclusions on the results of certain testing that could be administered at time of initial hiring interviews. Those results supposedly allow an employer to project which candidates for a position of employment are more or less likely to steal from you. There are other more authoritative sources that focus on this area.

One of the purposes of this book is to make you, the employer, think more deeply about the subject of employee dishonesty. After all, I have read where the amount of total loss from employee theft is over ten billion a year. That is a lot of money, and it all does not come from million dollar losses you read about in the paper. Based on my experiences, you have a lot of small and moderate size losses in that figure. Whether you operate a small business, moderate size professional practice or medium to large corporation, employee theft can adapt itself to the size of your company and cause you, and your company, financial problems in direct ratio to the financial exposure of your business. In other words, it may be just as important from a profit stand point of a small liquor store to find a $15,000 loss over ten months as it would be for a large hospital to find a $140,000 in two years. It may be just as difficult to find the theft in either the liquor store or in the hospital. Why? It is because the theft is not obvious, from a financial loss, when considering the thefts took place over a period of time.

Furthermore, no one felt that these losses would be possible in their respective businesses. Certainly, if an employee walked into a liquor store office, found the safe open and stole $15,000 at one time, it would have a tremendous effect on the cash operation of the store. Likewise, a theft of the cashier's office in the hospital of $140,000 at one time would cause serious financial problems. But as I have written, employee theft usually does not work that way.

Lets examine these losses a little more.

*CASE HISTORY: The liquor store had sales of over $250,000 annually. This loss of $15,000 was a combination of theft of money from the cash register, by ringing up **"no sales"** when a customer paid in cash, and the employee taking that amount out later in the shift, and by selling inventory to friends for a discount. An example would be the "customer" buys a half gallon of scotch and another half gallon of whiskey, but is charged for only one of the half gallons by the employee working the cash register. If you divide $15,000 over ten months, it averages to $1,500 a month. The losses were small to begin with and grew larger as the thief's greed and confidence increased. But for simplicity, if you divide the loss evenly, $1,500 per month, with one employee working a forty hour shift per week or twenty days per month, he only had to steal $9.38 per hour, or $75.00 per day to reach $1,500. With these two schemes going, that was not hard to do. With management not doing inventory until the end of the year, the inventory shortage would not show up until then.*

CASE HISTORY: The hospital loss concerned the in-house accountant of 19 years. She stole $140,000 over two years by cre-

*ating false patient refund vouchers. She knew that with the large amount of annual sales of the hospital, the outside auditors would find the loss from this department to be **"immaterial"** in their audit. This means that the total sales from this department were below a certain threshold in relation to overall sales for the entire hospital. Because she was careful not to go over this threshold, questionable transactions were not investigated or audited further. This in-house accountant knew that the materiality level was $70,000 per year.*

Why did I digress about these two losses when the subject in this part of the chapter is "who is a thief and why"?. For three reasons:

First, the company level of an employee that steals can range from a clerk or cashier, as in the liquor store case, up to and into supervisory or management/professional positions as in the in-house accountant.

Second, although these losses took place over eight years ago, the same lack of controls still exist today. I investigated a loss very similar to the hospital case this year. The lack of controls was terrible.

Third, is apathy. No one felt those losses could take place then, and it seems that many feel it cannot happen today. Recently a large national insurance company that writes employee dishonesty coverage wanted to hold a seminar for area hospitals. There was no charge to attend. Forty five invitations were sent out, five responded. Although the invitations were sent to top management, four of the five that responded were going to send lower lever supervisors.

It seems to me that many in management do not believe employee theft can affect them, until it does. Then they ask me "where were you six months ago with this information?" Well, I am here now to tell you that employee theft is here in a big way, and **if you do not improve your knowledge of this subject, it is just a matter of time before you become a victim.**

Why do employees steal and who are they? Remember the 19 year hospital accountant. She was well liked. She had a great personnel file. She had no addictions of illegal drugs or gambling. But, she did want to insure her retirement, so she stole the money and bought real estate in the area. Here are some more examples:

- There was the accounting manager of over 13 years, well liked, many awards in his file, who stole over $200,000 to pay off credit card debt.
- A manager of a large medical facility, over 25 years with the same employer stole over $100,000 in personal purchases using a company credit card.
- There was a former president of a medium sized recreational corporation, who stole $100,000 in less than three years. He made an excellent appearance, was well liked but had a gambling problem.
- A supervisor of an accounts payable department of a national contractor stole $200,000 in only a few months. It started out to pay only one month's mortgage, but went on from there when her co-conspirator threatened to expose her to the employer when she said she wanted to stop.

I could go on with many more examples of sizeable thefts by employees you would not think fit the mold of employee theft. The reason, there really isn't one mold or pattern; patterns are only one thing you look at.

There is one characteristic that appears quite often in employee theft losses; **the larger losses usually involve an employee that you trusted.**

So "Who Steals and Why", I would have to say that the most likely persons to steal are those that are:

- In a position to have access to "CYA" items that I discussed before.
- Those that are in need of money over and beyond what they earn, not for vacations, but to support an addiction they have, or a life style they cannot maintain otherwise.
- Those employees that feel they are not paid what they feel they are worth, or feel that their pay is small in comparison to what top management makes in the company.

You can plug in almost any level of employee into the above paragraph. **Anyone that has access, motive and opportunity can be a thief.**

WHY EMPLOYEES DO NOT LEAVE:

As to why employees do not leave before they are caught.

- They feel that their scheme allows them to have a job and a second source of income.
- They cannot **afford** to leave the job that has allowed them this "second income" that they **need.**
- They have no idea if they can do the same thing in another job.
- They may feel that their scheme or plan will never be discovered.

As I said before, but it deserves repeating, the person you hired ten years ago may now be faced with pressures that could change their personality and ethics. That is why in order to protect your company, you must constantly re-evaluate your key employees, and the controls you have in place. In chapter 9 we begin to study those controls.

Chapter Nine

Management Controls

Pre-employment

If one can say that a topic in a book of this nature has a main or "heart of the matter chapter",this, and the following two chapters, would be it. Although every chapter in this study is important, **"Management Controls"** are the procedures put in place that should, if not completely prevent employee theft from occurring, at least decrease the possibility of the theft taking place, and allow for early detection of that theft.

This chapter will begin with the employers first contact with the prospective employee, the interview/ application, and proceed through the various ways that management can prevent or minimize employee theft and it's impact on the company.

INTERVIEW/APPLICATION:

I place these together because the employment interview should include a completed job application with it. The interviewer should have reviewed the application before the job applicant comes in for the interview. This way the interviewer will be able to ask certain questions while focusing on the applicant's response to that question.

A lot can be learned from the way someone responds to certain questions or how they sit or move around during questioning:

- If you see a large gap in time between employers, that could mean that the applicant does not want to show that he worked at a certain employer during this time period. If he was terminated for some improper activity, you may want to know that before hiring the applicant.

- How does the applicant react to your questions about his work history.
- Another response to look for is when you ask the applicant why he left previous jobs.
- One final question, is to ask the applicant "what will your past employer say **when** I call him".

If the interviewer is experienced, any major or obvious detrimental actions or comments by the applicant will be noticed and a decision not to hire will be relatively easy. But for the ones that get hired, **"Management Controls"** have to be in place.

The second part of this section is the job application. It is important that a complete pre-form type application be used. You would be surprised how many times I have been asked to do an investigation only to find that one of the most important documents in that investigation, the employment application, was never completed. Why is it important? Because it gives the employer, and later, if there is a theft, the police or the insurance investigator important information about that employee.

Here is a summary of the items I would like to see in an application, and the reason for them. Compare it to what your company currently uses.

NAME:

You should ask for the complete name of the applicant along with any nicknames that he may have used. If the applicant is a female you should verify her maiden name. You do not know when she became married, and previous employers and back ground information may have her using her maiden name. Additionally, with so many people getting divorced, it is possible a woman would take back her previous name in that situation. This helps to try and identify the applicant's past, and assists in locating the employee in the future if needed.

DATE OF BIRTH/SOCIAL SECURITY NUMBER:

Most applications have these. But some employers do not verify that what is being given is correct. These help in making sure that the person under investigation is not someone else with a similar or identical name.

DRIVER'S LICENSE:

Very few applications request this form of ID. I feel it is very important because it not only provides you with a document from which you can verify name, date of birth and address, but it also will provide what you need in order to obtain a copy of the applicant's driving record. Most states will allow anyone with proper credentials, to obtain a job applicant's driving record. This could provide the employer with additional information on who they are considering hiring. For example, if the driving record shows DWI charges you may want to inquire on the history of this employee. If there is a drinking problem, that could be indicative of problems that could eventually lead to employee theft. Obviously, if the driving record shows any drug arrest you probably would not want to give that applicant any further consideration. (See below under discussion about disabilities.)

Should an employee leave your employment and change addresses, the license number provides access to any new address, or from an assets standpoint documents can be reviewed that verify what vehicles are registered in that person's name.

REFERENCES:

These are divided into two sections, personal and past employment. Personal references are seldom the source of important information. Any applicant would never use a reference if he or she thought the reference would give negative information about the applicant; however, it is a source of information should the employee needed to be located. In this case the reference is usually someone that is either a friend or relative, but if the right questions are asked you can sometimes gain information that can help in locating the employee.

The past employment history on the other hand can yield many items of information. You should always have enough space in the application for a five year employment history. Make sure that the dates from one employer to the other are connected. For example, if an employee left one employer on January 15th, the next employment should begin within two weeks, if not you should find out why.

Be certain to obtain names of the Personnel manager, Human Resources or General Manager of the previous employers. These are the persons who would most likely know if there was a problem with the applicant's past history.

It would seem that the amount of information a past employer provides would be in direct relation to the type of employee the applicant was. If the applicant was a good employee that left on good terms for either family transfer or a better position, the past employer will provide volumes of information on that employee. However, if the employee left on bad terms you will not be given much information. At least **you should not** be given much information. Sometimes employers do not know when they should say little or nothing about a past employee.

CASE HISTORY: An investigation of employee theft concerned a parts manager that was stealing parts received from vendors, and destroying or diverting the invoices from these vendors. Eventually the employee was caught, gave a verbal confession and was terminated before our involvement. The employer did not want to prosecute. When I asked the manager of the company what he would say to employers that might call inquiring about the employee's termination, he said he would tell the people who called exactly what the employee did.

Those statements could result in a lawsuit against the employer, because the employee was never convicted of the theft, and a verbal confession would probably be insufficient documentation of the employee's dishonesty in a civil trial brought by the employee for libel or slander.

From my experience as an insurance investigator of personal injury cases such as libel, slander or wrongful discharge it is my opinion that the courts have a tendency to lean in favor of the employee. Therefore the employer has to be very careful how he handles an employee during any discharge situation, or when there are inquires into that past employment history. **Remember, although the truth is the best defense in a libel or slander case, it is often difficult to prove.**

If you receive little information from the past employer about an applicant's history you should be able to "read between the lines". If the past employer only tells you the dates the person worked and what their job title was you should be on alert. If you ask the past employer would she rehire the employee and she says no, should **you** hire them?

DISQUALIFYING APPLICANTS:

When you do not want to hire someone because of his or her work or personal history, you want to make sure you are on solid ground in that rejection to hire. You have to take into account the EEOC (Equal Employment Opportunity Commission), and the "American's with Disability Act". Concerning the ADA regulations, it has been explained to me that people with drug or alcohol addictions can claim that these are disabilities. The applicant has to claim that **they** have a disability. **You** do not have to assume that the applicant is claiming that their addiction is a disability, nor do you have to ask if they are claiming any disability.

Always check with the Director of Human Resources in your company, or your state EEOC office or other state laws on not hiring someone because of an addiction or history of addiction. Obviously, it is always better from your company standpoint to refuse to hire someone based on a job ability related concern. For example, if you are looking for a typist that types ninety words a minute and the person you are interviewing only types sixty words a minute, that person probably could not object to not being hired. You should give the applicant a job description of the job they are applying for, **before any meeting,** then in the interview ask them if there are any reasons why they feel they could not do that job.

PAST CRIMINAL HISTORY:

Before adding this section to any job application you should check with your attorney or the local EEOC chapter to be certain what criminal history current law allows to be asked. There are certain questions that are no longer allowed. However, the question of past conviction for a theft is allowed, and this is the one question that focuses on the employee theft or dishonesty issue. You should recall a previous chapter where I discussed the coverage and exclusions under an "Employee Dishonesty Policy". Any dishonest action by the employee in the past, that is discovered by or known to the current employer voids the coverage for that employee, under most bond policies. If you have that question on the application you will know whether the employee can be bonded. Of course the employee may not put down the truth concerning his history but at least the question is there. Remember, there is no exclusion of coverage if the employee lies about his history and the employer does not find out about it before a new theft occurs. But, if the applicant responds that he or she **has** such a history, you should make sure anyone responsible for hiring knows what that history could mean, in relation to the coverage and the ability to bond the employee. If the bond policy wording is not known by the person doing the hiring, it could cost the company considerable money should a theft take place. (Remember the case discussed in Chapter 3 about the hotel night auditor)?

I have had several insurance agents ask me that if the insured is not penalized by not knowing the dishonest history of the employee, what is the advantage of placing a "Criminal History" type question in the application. The reason, as I have written earlier, is you may not want to take a chance on hiring someone that may steal from you. If they have a history of dishonesty, are they likely to do it again? If they do, that loss is not covered. And the unreimbursed cost to the company for the process of discovery, proving and prosecuting an employee dishonesty loss can be substantial and should be avoided if possible. Remember the Health Care facility that spent over $15,000 to an outside auditing firm to **prove** the loss for the insurance company. That amount was not recoverable under the policy nor were the many hours spent with staff during my investigation.

Some states allow employers to request criminal convictions from that state. In Maryland, an employer pays a fee to the state for this service and makes the written inquiry as needed. Bear in mind, with bonding companies not requiring criminal prosecution under most policies, you could hire someone with a history of dishonesty that simply was never recorded. That is why the other parts of the application are so important.

This concludes the sections in the application that I believe are important in the protection to the employer. Other sections that concern themselves with salary requirements and previous positions or the type position the applicant is applying for are normally not part of our study.

However, there are additional comments about applications that are important. One concerns temporary employees. Generally, you, as the employer rely on the "temp" agency to screen the people that they are sending out to employers like yourself. You should not count too heavily on the depth of their interviews. In my chapter on "Who is covered" I discussed that "temp" employees come under your bond policy as long as they are under your supervision and the loss occurs on your property. Yet, you may not know anything about that employee's history. My suggestion is that you ask for a copy of that "temps" application and that you ask the type questions you would normally ask someone that you were going to hire as a regular employee of your company. This may take more time than you would like to spend on a temporary employee, but the time is well spent, even if the position is not a critical or important one. **Remember, a thief does not always have to have direct access to your money to steal from you.** Finally, complete applications on all employees are important not only for information on the employee that is involved in a theft, but also on employees that may be important to an investigation, but have changed jobs since the loss occurred and the time it was discovered. There have been a number of cases where I needed to find past employees to verify what was going on in a certain department or be a witness in our investigation on other employees. Having as much information as possible would make finding someone a little easier.

BACKGROUND CHECKS:

By this I mean having a professional (usually a Private Investigation Agency) look into the history of someone in an in depth manner. There are investigative agencies in every state that have the experience and access to obtain numerous documents on an applicant's background. As the employer you have to decide if the position being filled and the exposure to the company justify the cost of the background check. The checks on a payroll clerk for example would not be as extensive as those on a Vice President of Finance. These checks can cost from several hundred to several thousand dollars depending on what you wish to be covered in the investigation.

PERSONNEL SCREENING:

There are two types of screening that may be helpful in determining, at the applicant level, whether that applicant could be a future thief. These are the **"Written Honesty Test"** and **"Handwriting (Graphology) Analysis"**. I have had no experience with these tests in my years as an investigator of employee theft losses. No employer has ever provided me with results of any personnel test that showed the person I was investigating for employee theft now, was found at the time of being hired, prone to the type of personality or had character flaws that would tend to make the person a possible thief. Very few employers that I have worked with, admitted using these tests in their consideration of an applicant. From my readings, I know these methods are being used, but I am not qualified to comment on their effectiveness.

I only add these methods as another control that management may consider using in an effort to weed out hiring someone that may steal from them in the future. Your Director of Human Resources is the best person to inquire of these tests.

There are several comments that I will make that management must consider before using these tests. First, both tests are legal. There are no laws broken by asking an applicant to submit to a honesty test. The graphology analysis simply requires more than a signature for the expert to render an opinion, so you as the employer have to obtain several sentences in order for the analysis to be fair.

Both methods require a subjective interpretation of the results, more so for the handwriting than for the other test.

Finally you have to ask whether these tests are an indication of the applicant's personality and character based on their life style, monetary concerns and stresses today, or are the results indicative of a personality shaped over a lifetime. I make these statements because I have seen so many long term employees go bad after many years of having a positive work history, I wonder if a test given say ten years ago is going to reflect a true picture of the employee today.

LIE DETECTOR TEST:

Since the Employee Polygraph Protection Act of 1988 (EPPA) polygraph or lie detector exams are seldom used for job applicants. I have been advised that some exceptions to this law exist concerning jobs that are with the federal government, state or local government, as well as occupations in money, weapons or pharmaceutical type occupations.

As to the use of polygraph exams in the course of an employee theft investigation, the federal law **allows you to ask** if the employee will take the test. But you can not force an employee to take it, nor can you fire them if they do not take it. To be safe, check with the

States Attorney's Office in your state for an updated opinion on how your state feels about these test.

DRUG SCREENING:

I understand that it is quite common for many employers, across a wide spectrum of industries, to require applicants for hire to take a urine test to rule out any drug dependency. Please check with the laws in your state concerning these tests.

This concludes the pre-hiring controls. Now in chapter ten, we start an in depth study on methods of theft and the controls that should be in place to stop all employee theft.

Chapter Ten

Methods of Theft
and
Management Controls
(After hiring)

Checkbook, Accounts payable, Fraudulent Vendors & Invoices, Services, Expense Accounts, Receivables & Inventory.

In the next two chapters I will discuss the type of controls that if put into effect, would easily reduce employee theft by over fifty percent. Additionally, any loss that might occur would be reduced by thousands of dollars because the loss would be discovered much earlier. Some of these controls are discussed in almost every risk consultant's or auditor's remarks, be they in a seminar, or after an audit by an auditing firm. Sometimes the wording used in describing the controls may differ but the meanings are the same.

To provide the reader with a clear understanding of this subject, I have incorporated any discussion of **"Management Controls"** with examples of the **"Methods of Theft"** that those controls, if in place and followed, could have aided in the discovery of the theft early into the embezzlement, and in many cases actually prevented the loss from occurring.

I will go into detail on several of these methods of theft so one can see how the theft was done. Any in depth discussion will be on cases that I investigated. I will first list the type of theft or exposure, followed by examples of the theft and then the controls that should have been in place. Finally I will write about the businesses or industries that are prone to this type of theft.

THEFT FROM CHECKBOOK, BANK STATEMENT & ACCOUNTS PAYABLE:

This has been one of the most common methods of theft that I have investigated. One would think that it would be easy to control, and it is, but for some reason it comes up time after time, year after year.

CASE HISTORY: Around 1989 I investigated a loss involving employee theft from a doctor's office. This was a small group of two doctors and two clerical staff. The long term manager decided to retire, so Mary was promoted to that position. Several months after Mary was in place, one of the doctors realized that their cash flow was short, so he asked Mary what the problem was. Mary advised that the patients were not paying. The doctor told her to send out more overdue payment letters to patients. Mary said she would, but she did not. Another month went by with no further investigation by the doctor. One day Mary called in sick, and did not return for several days. The doctors asked Helen to come in while Mary was out. While Helen was working, the bank statement came in. When Helen examined the statement and the checks in the statement, she found many checks written to Mary as payee. Those checks totaled much more than Mary's salary would support. After reviewing other months, they found a pattern of theft that was going on for about six months which totaled about $40,000.

Mary's method of theft was simple. She would pay herself many times a month, with each check in amounts of several hundred dollars. She forged the same doctor's name on the checks. The one doctor had a signature that consisted of several loops only and was quite easy to forge. When the bank statement came in she would open it and remove all checks that she had made payable to herself. One by one she would do the following with the checks. She would "white out" her name as payee and make a copy of that check. She would discard the original cancelled check. She would take her first copy and write in a payee that would be recognized as a vendor or accounts payable of the practice, and make a copy of that check. She would discard the first copy. She would place the second copy in the bank state-

ment envelope, and on the check book stub for that numbered check write in the payee that matched what she had written on the second copy.

As you read this, you are probably thinking why didn't the doctor simply review the bank statement and the checks. By doing this he would have seen several copies of checks that did not match the color of real cancelled checks, as well as seeing payments to Mary for much more than her salary. I asked the doctor why he did not do this. He advised me that it never occurred to him that an employee would steal from him. I have heard this comment countless times.

As I wrote in an earlier chapter, the wonderful employee you hired years ago, may be robbing you blind today. As an employer, Managing Partner, Risk Manager, etc. you have to accept the fact that there are employees that turn bad and for many reasons steal from their employers. You must take the emotion out of this relationship and make decisions on sound business principles.

For those who are interested, Mary had a cocaine problem. She wasn't worried about her employer's cash flow, she was more concerned about having the money for her next **"buy"**.

It isn't always a drug or gambling addiction that makes an employee steal,nor is this type of theft from the check book limited to small practices or businesses.

CASE HISTORY: Recently I concluded an investigation involving a large hospital. This facility had revenues of over $200 million per year and should have had available the resources to construct the best internal controls possible. However, this was not the case. In this incident, the accounting manager began taking the first two checks off of the continuous feed accounts payable runs, typing his name as payee, writing the checks for several thousand dollars each time, and depositing the checks into his personal account. Apparently the first two checks placed into the printer were used only to start the runs, they were blank when they came out of the printer, meaning no accounts payable payee's name appeared.

The employee would void the check numbers in the accounts payable check log. He then ran the checks through the check signing machine, which would place one officer's name on the checks. Two signatures were required for certain amounts, but the employee knew to keep the amount of the checks under that limit, that way, no one had to see that the checks were payable to him.

The "work" was done early in the morning before anyone else came to the office. This theft went on for nine years, totaling over $200,000 dollars. Why wasn't it caught sooner? One reason is that the manager was also in charge of reconciling the bank statement for the facility. When the bank statement came in, he would remove the checks and discard them, and would make journal entries to cover the amount of the checks, and make the reconciliation balance to the general ledger.

When I met with the employee he advised that it wasn't gambling or drugs, or fancy cars that made him a thief, it was just the fact that his family's live style required more money than he made. Since he was an accountant, he knew how to hide the money in such a way that the hospital's revenues, in relation to what he stole, would make it unlikely that any audit would be detailed enough to trace the money. The reason for that was the amount of money stolen per year, was on average about $35,000, which fell below what is "material" in relation to the overall sales of $200 million per year. Finally, he knew that there were no controls in place that would allow his scheme to be discovered.

In this type of theft the employee either writes his name as payee, as shown above, or writes the name of another person or company as payee and the employee writes that payee's name on the back. He then writes his or her own name as a second endorsee and negotiates the check. When the check is returned, it is usually pulled from the other checks and discarded.

In another method, the employee will take checks that have already been filled out with a legitimate payee name and have it signed by the proper officer of the company and then erase or lift off the payee's name and place their own name as payee and negotiate the check. You may be thinking that this could not go on for long because soon the legitimate payee would want to be paid. However, in a few months, thousands of dollars can be taken before the loss is discovered.

CASE HISTORY: A contractor had a very successful season and there was good cash flow. The owner was busy with projects and the responsibilities of operating a $1.5 million dollar operation. The bookkeeper had developed a drug problem and due to that, stole over $40,000 in just over three months. The employee stole in several ways; by paying herself extra checks and forging the owners signature; by having the owner sign blank checks after which she would make payments to herself; and by taking actual account payable checks, properly signed by the owner, and lifting off the payee's name and placing her own in the same spot.

TYPE OF CONTROLS:

"Separation or segregation of duties", is one of the controls that should have been in place. Under auditor's wording this would mean that the person who pays the bills for the company, partnership or corporation should not be the one that balances the checkbook or reconciles the bank statement. It is too easy for that person to alter the books in ways that theft is easy, detection sometimes difficult and the results devastating to the company. This is especially important if you have someone with an accounting or finance background. They have the training and practical experience to know how to hide stolen money through a series of accounting entries, and they are going to know what outside auditors look for in any audits performed.

"Supervision of bank statement reconciliation" is the second control that is needed. If employees in positions that give them access to steal know that their work is being reviewed on a regular basis they are going to be less inclined to steal using those methods. This also applies to managers or people that have earned respect and position based on years of solid work performance. **Senior management must always have someone looking over the work of employees and managers, because sometimes legitimate errors are made and sometimes people you trust go bad.**

"Never sign blank checks" is a third control that belongs here. You should never be in such a hurry that you cannot find the time to have the completed checks presented to you **"before"** you sign your name. The time you think you are saving by signing blank checks today, could cost you a hundred times more if you have to meet with someone like myself in a bond loss investigation.

The following additional **"controls"** should be considered as well.

"The employee that presents checks for signature, should not be the one that mails them out" In other words someone else should place them in the envelope for payment. If possible select an employee that does not have access to the checkbook or the computer accounts payable software. This way you minimize the chance that someone would lift off the correct payee's name and replace it with their own.

"Check for forgeries" An employee could copy (forge) your signature good enough to pass your bank's "verification department". Occasionally check your signature. To make forgeries more difficult, your signature should be legible, not some fancy combination of loops or lines that can be easily forged.

"Check off check numbers that appear in the bank statement" against the physical checks in your possession. Simply looking for proper payees or the authenticity of your signature on those checks in your statement does not account for any checks that have been removed by the thief before you see that bank statement.

"Checks should be kept in a locked compartment" is the final control. Access to and the keys or combination of that compartment should only be given to a few trusted employees. To do otherwise can cause problems. Remember the temporary employee who worked only a few days, but in that time found the checkbook and took several checks **from the back of the checkbook**, cashed them and stole $12,000? That could have been avoided.

TYPES OF BUSINESS:

As to the type businesses that these methods of theft and controls apply to, **"EVERY COMPANY HAS A CHECKBOOK OR ACCOUNTS PAYABLE"** to pay their bills. Whether it is a two person firm or a large corporation with hundreds of employees, somehow bills have to be paid. The exposure is there for every type of company in every industry.

The only safe company is the one person operation where he or she writes his or her own checks. They certainly are not going to steal from themselves. But as soon as the company grows and the owner allows someone else to write checks, an exposure is created and some sort of control should be put in place and adhered to.

THEFT FROM ESCROW OR OPEN ACCOUNTS:

This method is similar to the above but I have separated it because these losses usually involve large service type accounts. In these cases, the amount of money in the reserve account that the checks are drawn on is considerable. Second, there is usually a lot of activity on these accounts, meaning that many checks are written, perhaps from several origins. Third, reconciliation of the accounts are slow because there is either so much activity on the account, making reconciliation difficult and time consuming, or the checks go to a main office, sometimes in a different city or state. The theft is usually done in one of three ways: First, is the employee that writes checks from an open escrow account and charges the amount to one of the files that the office services.

CASE HISTORY: One case involved the manager of a Real Estate Title Company. Title Companies have an escrow or trust account from which all payments are made, and that payment is to be off-

set by the appropriate debit to that particular case. After a settlement, the settlement attorney makes disbursements from the proceeds, as an example: to real estate brokers, contractors and taxes or other charges. This manager began writing checks payable to the bank that was used by the title company. This was done after the property settlement took place. Since she had signature authority and was known by the bank, she was able to either have the funds cashed or deposited into her own account. She then debited the settlement papers with that expenditure. From the review of the files, settlements that had a large number of expenditures were her choice. In review of these cases sometimes the credits and debits balanced out, other times there was a deficit. It was the deficits that eventually brought discovery of the theft, but only after many months had gone by.

The second method is to add the "employee" name to legitimate payees that are due checks from the employer.

CASE HISTORY: A clerk in a medical facility that processed checks to patients or other medical providers, stole money by adding her name as a payee. The theft was simple to see because the workmanship was crude. The employee's typed name differed from the type used to print the correct payees name. The embezzler signed the payee's name on the back of the check and then signed her name. She then deposited the check into her savings account.

The third method involves an employee that is supposed to refund money to customers or patients after a company or medical facility is paid by another source, such as an insurance company.

CASE HISTORY: A hospital had a 20 year employee steal a large sum of money by creating false accounts payable checks to fictitious hospital patients. The employee had a long work history and was well liked in the accounting and finance office of the hospital. She began her theft by thinking up fictitious patient names, putting the names on an accounts payable form with the heading of "patient refund". She sent this to the accounting office and requested that the check be brought back to her. The employee then forged or signed the name of the "patient" on the back of the check, and signed her own name or the name of a co-conspirator and deposited the check into a bank account.

The checks were to be reviewed by a supervisor before they were sent out. The investigation found that at least some of the checks were initialed by the supervisor, but there was never any questioning of the "employee" by the supervisor.

This loss involved nearly 200 checks written in less than two years time. The checks would vary in amount from $200 to $800 dollars. The grand total was over a $140,000.

In the case where checks were made payable to a company, the bank should never have allowed those checks to be deposited into a personal accounts. Banking regulations require that any check made payable to a company or business must be deposited in that business account. In this case, either the teller did not know the regulations or waived them because the teller knew the employee as a good customer.

As to the clerk working for the medical facility, when her theft was discovered, the bonding company and in turn myself were called in immediately. By working with insurance company retained attorneys we were able to freeze funds at the bank where the employee did business. The employee was prosecuted, found guilty and spent several years in jail.

In the case of the in-house hospital accountant, she had used the money to buy investment property in the area. The hospital was successful in freezing assets before they turned the matter over for prosecution. The employee/ defendant was placed on five years probation but not governed by restitution for what she stole. According to the record, the defalcator violated her probation, was found guilty and the probation continued. As far as I can determine she was never incarcerated for her theft from the hospital.

TYPES OF CONTROLS:

Sometimes no matter what controls are in place they are not going to stop theft. However, if in place, controls would have kept those above losses to a minimum. Lets examine those cases for those controls.

"Perform a timely reconciliation of the escrow account" refers to the matter of the title company. Whenever there is a theft by a person in management, it is usually costly because they are already in charge and thought to be above the level of a thief. There wasn't anyone in the office to review the checks that the manager was writing. However, there were clerks in the main office whose job duties included reconciliation. However, they were behind and did not do their job. Had the clerks done their job, the loss would have been discovered much earlier and in turn the loss would have been smaller.

"Supervisor's review of work" refers to the clerk that added her name as payee. After the checks were completed by the clerk, the checks should have been reviewed by a supervisor and been given to someone else for mailing. This again is an example of **"separation of duties"**.

"Loss control procedures meetings or written instructions" refers to the in-house accountant. There was a control in place, with the supervisor looking over the work before it was sent out. For whatever reason, that supervisor did not catch the fraud. The hospital should have made sure supervisors knew what documents were needed regardless of who was making the request.

"An internal auditor" should have reviewed the account on a quarterly basis. By checking the supervisor's work this loss would have been much smaller.

TYPES OF BUSINESS:

What types of companies would be susceptible to these methods of theft? **"TITLE COMPANIES** and **"MEDICAL FACILITIES"** are susceptible. So are **"INSURANCE, INVESTMENT AND FINANCIAL INSTITUTIONS** . . . any service oriented company that issues large volume of checks.

THEFT FROM FICTITIOUS VENDORS OR FRAUDULENT INVOICES:

This type of theft is usually done by an employee that is either in charge of an accounts payable department or has management status. If the theft is being perpetrated by the supervisor or individual in charge of ordering payments to accounts payable, they probably have computer access, since the majority of companies pay bills with computer generated payments.

If the theft is being accomplished by someone in management, it would most likely be someone that would have a position with the company where vendors send their invoices to that manager, so he or she could "**approve**" his or her own invoice for payment as well as legitimate ones.

The theft begins with the employee generating a false invoice either from his or her computer at work or from his or her home. You have probably seen legitimate invoices from vendors that were elementary in creativity and design. With today's computer software, professional looking invoices and bills are even easier to do. Once the invoice is either created at work or mailed to the attention of the supervisor or manager running this scheme, it is taken to accounts payable for payment.

CASE HISTORY: The first case involved the building division accounts payable clerk for a large national construction company. Donna, the employee, had been working there several years and had a good work record. She was married with a family. One month she was short on cash and did not have enough money for bills. She thought of a way to generate some additional income.

As the accounts payable clerk, it was her job to review all invoices from sub-contractors that worked for her employer, the general contractor. She would review all paperwork that supported the invoices. Included, was the need for an "authorization to pay stamp". Once everything was in order, she would put the request for payment in the computer and it would be sent to the accounting department where the checks would be issued.

Donna's scheme was simple, she took a plain piece of paper and wrote the name of a vendor, with a date and amount for services rendered. The vendor's name was that of her cousin. She had previously contacted her relative and told him what she was going to do. She asked if he wanted part of the money and he said he did. After typing the invoice, she placed an approval stamp on it, keyed it into the system and waited for the check to be cut.

After waiting for a certain period of time Donna went down to the office where the checks were issued and picked them up. Once work was over for that day, she met her cousin, gave him the check and he deposited it into his bank account. Shortly thereafter, the money was withdrawn and they split it fifty-fifty.

When I met with the Donna, she advised that she was going to do this only one time. However, she said her cousin called her, remarked how easy it was and wanted to do it again. When she said no, he threatened to go to her employer. In the next few months nine more checks were issued with a total amount around $200,000.

Most checks were issued payable to the cousin and his fictitious company, and a few checks were payable to a friend of the cousin. Donna says she only received a small percentage of the money because she wanted to stop and did not want the money anymore.

This theft was very interesting for two reasons. First, there was so much money stolen so easily and so quickly, plus the employee that started it wanted to stop but could not because of fear she would be exposed. Second, the FBI became involved because the checks were being written on a bank that was out of state. (It wasn't often that I had an investigation that involved federal officials, but whenever I did, it was always a pleasure working with them.)

The result of the theft was that the employee was found guilty and, according to one of the officer's of the company, was given an 18 month sentence. The cousin was also found guilty and given a jail sentence.

The second case involved someone in management.

CASE HISTORY: *You may recall a case I discussed briefly in chapter 2. It involved the manager of the new car prep department for a car dealer. He would first steal a little, and as his confidence grew, steal more. The facts were that the employee was hired in the latter months of 1989 as a new car prep manager. The first **"invoice"** from his **"own company"** was dated in May of 1990 for several hundred dollars of supplies. According to the dealer the invoice was mailed to the manager's attention. Subsequent invoices showed that the invoices increased in number, being dated every other day or so. Then during the summer, July through September they stopped, only to start again in the fall with heavier **"sales"** to the dealership.*

The manager had the invoices mailed to his attention at the dealership. He would walk the invoice over to the accounts payable clerk and ask her to pay it. Since he was the manager, the clerk was not in a position to question the validity of the request.

The embezzlement continued through the winter and spring of 1991 ending in May when the dealer discovered the scheme. In speaking to the dealer, he informed me that the employee was found guilty but never spent any time in jail.

As you are reading these cases you may be thinking to yourself, are these examples exceptions, or are these types of losses something that could happen to any employer. During the writing of this chapter I read in the paper of an executive with a large national company that produces grain products, allegedly being found guilty of embezzling over 9 million dollars by submitting false invoices. Here is one of largest companies in the world, with enough assets to surely have in place "internal controls" and yet the company claims they lost nine million to this employee.

THEFT BY A GHOST EMPLOYEE:

I placed this method of theft here because this type of theft can be found in any large employee based corporation or governmental agency. This is a **"non-existent employee"** that is thought up by someone in a supervisory or higher position. The perpetrator then fills out payroll documents, and personnel information and starts getting a paycheck in that employees name. (I have never had this type of investigation, but I have read about them. A recent theft was by a woman that held a high position in a city government and began sending paychecks, made out to a fake name, to an address that she owned under a company name).

Any payments would be in checks that would have to be endorsed over to the real employee.

TYPES OF CONTROLS:

In the Donna's theft there were several **"lack of controls"** that allowed this loss to continue.

"Standard invoice document procedures" should have been in place with the accounts payable office. That office should have requested supporting paperwork attached to those invoices backing up the payment requested. Since Donna was creating the invoices from the computer at her desk, she would have had a hard time supplying any back up.

"List of approved vendors" should have been with the accounts payable office, **"supplied by upper management"**. This would have sent a signal to any employees or department managers contemplating theft, that they would not be successful in submitting false vendor invoices. (This was also the main control missing in the case of the auto dealer new car prep manager).

"Separation of duties" is the final control. The clerk that requested payment should not have been allowed to pick up the completed check.

The loss was discovered by a control that was in place:

"Review of account or job expenditures". Donna knew that she had to charge the amount she was stealing to a job that was being worked on. The foreman on one such job notified the home office when he saw a payment to a sub-contractor he did not recognize as being on that job. When the home office looked into the matter, the scheme was uncovered.

As to the ghost employee, without specific controls, this is a difficult loss to uncover for three reasons. First, the person that has to plant the **"ghost employee"** must be an employee in at least a supervisory position. They already have status, respect, and are usually not questioned by someone under them. Second, this type of fraud only works where there are many employees working in several departments. People may see a name and never wonder why they haven't met that person. The large number of employees make it is easier to have someone that is never around. Third, the payroll system would be one where checks are sent to the ghost employee's home address, not picked up at work. This would be the address where the real employee goes to pick up the checks. It would not be difficult for someone with authority to start an employee file and send a memo to payroll and request a salary for the new employee.

"Rostering the payroll" is the best way to control this type of theft. Upper management arranges to have a manager of one department, **"meet and speak with"** all people listed on payroll records of another department. This accomplishes several things:

- Verify no "ghost employees".
- Update personnel records: addresses phone numbers, marital status, etc.
- Obtain one on one input from the employee on how things are going.

TYPES OF BUSINESS:

They are too numerous to mention, however general categories would be: **COMPANIES WITH ACCOUNTS PAYABLE,** as well as those that have **VENDORS THAT SUPPLY GOODS, SERVICES OR EQUIPMENT** that the company needs to stay in business.

THEFT OF RECEIVABLES/ DONATIONS OR FEES:

This theft occurs when an employee steals money that is payable to his or her employer for services or equipment provided by their employer. It can also include theft of donations, if it is a non-profit association, or fees that come from members or other persons. The majority of payments are by check, usually received in the mail and once received should be deposited into the checking or savings account of the employer.

There are two methods of theft. The first, requires the employee to add his or her name as an additional payee to a check that is meant for the employer, sign the employer's name on the back of the check and sometimes write, **"payable to the 'employee name'"**. This would be a two party check. The "employee" takes the check to his or her bank for deposit in his account. In some cases the employee would just endorse the back, not even adding his or her name to the payee part on the front of the check.

CASE HISTORY: A salesman for a computer software company was able to get his employer's clients to allow him to pick up payments that were payable to the employer for computer services. The salesman took the checks, usually in amounts of $2000 to $4500 to his bank, and was able to deposit the checks into his personal account. On some of the checks he added his name, other checks he did not, he just signed his name or account number on the back.

This is another example where the bank should not have allowed a deposit into a personal account. I remember some of those checks. The payee was clearly a company name, on the back were the initials of the company (written by the employee) and the signature of the employee, and his account number.

In case you are wondering what happened, the salesman was caught and prosecuted. The bank he did business with was presented a subrogation claim by the bonding company. The bonding company settled with the bank.

The second method was a new one for me, and I thought very creative.

CASE HISTORY: *The employee worked for a national association that received annual fees from agents wanting to represent association's members. The employee's job was to post the payments, and deposit them into the associations's account. This association was well known by it's initials and most payments would show those initials in the "pay to the order of" part of the check. The employee opened a checking account for a company whose initials matched the initials or acronym of the national association. When payments in the office of the association were received, instead of depositing them in the association account, he took them to his bank.*

This employee was hired in 1993 and began his theft in the fall of 1994. In the span of four months he had embezzled over $70,000. Because the theft was of union fees, it was considered a federal crime and the FBI became involved.

As a result of his theft, the employee entered a plea bargain with the government, was ordered to pay back what was stolen at a rate of several hundred dollars per month and was incarcerated. The length of time is not known by me, but I have been informed he is no longer in jail.

TYPE OF CONTROLS:

"Set accounts receivable procedures" would have been a "control" in the theft by the computer salesman. The office knew after several weeks that payments were not being received. When confronted, the salesman had excuses to explain why the money had not been turned in. If the above "control" had been in place and followed, the loss would have been discovered quickly. This loss lasted many months. Someone in the office who was tracking the accounts receivables should have realized there was a problem as soon as they contacted a client and found out the client paid the invoice that the office was calling about. Instead the salesman was able to keep this going for awhile before finally being discovered.

"Separation of duties" would have stopped the loss from the national professional association. Whomever opens the mail should not be the same person that prepares the checks for deposit. Likewise another person should be making that deposit.

If "separation of duties" is not put in place, the situation is perilous because there are no invoices to check against receivables as a regular profit making entity would have. The association or non-profit group relies on fees and donations that do not come in on a regular basis. Therefore a control as above is needed.

TYPES OF BUSINESS:

ANY BUSINESS, PARTNERSHIP, ASSOCIATION OR NON-PROFIT GROUP, that is paid for services or receives donations or fees by mail is vulnerable.

THEFT FROM EXPENSE ACCOUNT / COMPANY CREDIT CARDS:

There is nothing difficult to understand about this type of theft. An employee of the company is given a company credit card to use when on company business and an expense associated with that work is incurred. The theft takes place when the employee charges an expense on the card that he or she knows is not company related. You have an employee that is, in essence, receiving some sort of goods or service, that is over the salary and benefits of that employee. The employer pays that expense when the credit card company bills the employer for that charge.

As to the expense account theft, this takes place when the employee submits an expense that has already been paid by the employer. Here is one example that involves both types of thefts.

CASE HISTORY: A medical facility had a large number of volunteers that worked for them. To help moral and assist in everyone knowing each other better, the facility had an office that would arrange trips for the volunteers and anyone else that wanted to go. With the assistance of a professional travel agency, trips to cities throughout the U.S. would be arranged.

The credit card was used to pay for major expenses on the trip. When everyone returned, those that had not paid in advance would pay the office that arranged the trip. The credit card was issued in the name of the facility and the employee that was in charge of coordinating the trips. While on these trips and while making what appears to be personal visits to many cities in the country, the employee bought personal items and charged them on the credit card. These personal items would consist of hotel charges, meals, clothing, jewelry. In reviewing the receipts of purchases it was obvious that there were a large number of articles that were not expenses the facility should have been charged with.

This theft went on for several years. When finally discovered, an audit was completed by an outside auditing firm. The total for what the auditors considered were expenses outside sanctioned travel was in excess of $60,000.

This same employee would take the monthly credit card receipts received by the credit card company, block out the account number of the facility and submit that receipt as back up to the employee's expense account report. For example, if there was a hotel charge as a result of a training seminar, the hotel charge would be billed to the credit card of the facility. When the credit card company sent their statement to the facility, it would come to the attention of this employee. The employee would make a copy of that receipt page, cross out the account number and attach that receipt to the expense account for that month or a later month. The employer was paying for the hotel room with the monthly credit card payment and paying the employee with the expense account, an expense that the employee never incurred. These "expenses" were submitted for at least five years.

This expense account loss was discovered after the credit card loss was looked into. It took many man hours for the accounting department to research their records. Preparation of the claim took away from regular medical accounting department duties as well. The end result was an additional loss of over $13,000, not including the cost of having to put the claim together.

At the time of writing this chapter, the employer is pursuing this loss through the criminal court system. The employee had retained an attorney and he would not allow me to interview his client. From the information obtained the bonding company made payments to their insured and are preparing subrogation. As to the criminal matter, that will be decided many months from now unless there is a plea bargain.

TYPE OF CONTROLS:

"Written acceptable credit card purchases and business expense instructions" is the first control. Whenever an employer provides a company credit card and or expense account, the employer should make certain that every employee who is going to receive a card or use the expense account sign that they know what is and isn't acceptable. This is just good management. I have had several cases where an employee used a credit card for what he or she thought was a legitimate expense only to have it rejected, and a small employee dishonesty claim made. Remember, if there was no indication of theft, the policy does not pay for loss as a result of poor business practice.

By having a written set of instructions that is given out and signed by those employees that have expense accounts and credit cards, there is a record of what is and what is not legitimate. Without something in writing, I could see an employee claiming that he did not realize that a certain charge he made was not something that everyone did. Of course reality and practicality come into play here. Charging a cruise on the company card, without authorization would be more than a stretch to belief the employee thought he or she was entitled to that perk.

"Supervisor's authorization" of both expense accounts and credit card usage is the next control that was not used. In the above case, the employee completed her own expense form and submitted it to accounts payable directly. In the matter of the credit card invoices the employee either walked it to accounts payable or sent it through inter office mail with a note that said "please pay".

No matter how many years the employee has worked in your company, no matter how high their position, there should always be someone over them to look over what they are submitting. In the above case, the fraudulent expense was so obvious anyone who looked at the paperwork would have realized the expenses were not legitimate. But, since the employee was well respected, and had been there many years, no one questioned what was submitted.

"Credit card company invoices should be sent to the accounting manager or upper management" is the next control. The monthly invoice should never be sent to the employee whose name is on the card. It really isn't the employee's card in the first place.

"Accounts payable or internal accounting /auditor review": The final control should have caught this theft early. Any employee hired to pay accounts payable and employee expense accounts should have a good idea what is acceptable and what isn't. The expenditures in this employee theft loss were blatant. It was the worst example of lack of internal controls, in this type of case, I had ever seen. When someone in accounts payable sees an expense account voucher, they are to check the amount claimed against the paperwork to back up that amount. If the paperwork shows white outs of credit card account numbers, and shows expenses that the employer would usually pay through a company credit card, but it is being submitted as an expense that the employee claims to have paid him or herself, questions should be asked.

Internal review is also necessary in the event you may have an employee and supervisor working together, for the dual purpose of stealing from the employer. This way the loss can be discovered before it becomes a monster.

TYPES OF BUSINESS:

EMPLOYERS THAT PROVIDE EMPLOYEE EXPENSE ACCOUNTS OR CREDIT CARDS are companies that are susceptible to this type of theft. Usually large employers with a busy accounts payable department may be more of a target.

THEFT OF INVENTORY AND SERVICES:

When the word "inventory" is used it is interchangeable with the word "stock". This method of theft involves either the direct theft of the employer's inventory by the employee, or schemes that allow that employee, usually working with other non-employee type individuals, to receive financial gain over and above legitimate salary, benefits etc.

As to theft of services, I place this in the same category as inventory because it is what the employer sells. A retailer has inventory, a caterer or repair facility has a service. The theft of either directly affects the ability of the company to make a profit. The methods used are as numerous as the various types of inventory and services found throughout industry. Furthermore, the thefts can come from either outside or inside stationed employees.

Theft by outside salespersons:

In these type of thefts, the employee is an outside salesperson or account representative who is supposed to sell goods or services of the employer to it's clients. If it is a theft of goods, the salesman has to make the delivery himself. If it is a theft of service it usually requires the employee to get the customer to make a change from the normal method that an account or order is processed. Here are examples of both.

CASE HISTORY: A large liquor wholesaler discovered a theft when one of their clients called for a meeting because the client's records reflected payments for liquor that the client did not receive. The owner of the wholesaler business contacted the account representative for that client and asked that he attend the meeting. Prior to the meeting the employee admitted that he had been stealing for many months.

The employee's method was simple. He took orders from his clients and then went to the warehouse and asked that the order be filled. He then placed the order in his car and took the liquor to sell it on the street. The salesman took the shipping or-

der that should have gone to the client, forged the signature of the person that normally received the goods, then turned the copy of the order into the office. The client was then billed by the office accounts receivable staff.

During my investigation I asked the controller why the clients paid the invoices before they made certain that the shipments were received. According to him the retail clients pay the bills as fast as possible so the wholesaler does not put them on a COD basis. With the invoice coming at a different time than the shipment, it makes it difficult for the retailer to match up that shipment with the invoice. Since inventories were only done yearly, it could be several months before the shortage would be discovered, if discovered at all.

According to the subrogation receipt signed by the controller for the wholesaler, the losses began in late 1992 and continued until May of 1994. Assuming that liquor retailers or bars and lounges that bought the product were on a calendar year for inventory and financial purposes, they would have gone through two inventories, end of 1992 and 1993, and it was not until May of '94 that one determined there was a problem. (It does not say much for their own controls does it. I suppose they just marked the loss as shrinkage, due either to unproven employee theft on their part or theft from **their** customers). The paid loss was over $20,000.

CASE HISTORY: A well known caterer submitted a claim for theft when clients were billed for services that they already paid for. The caterer received calls from clients that had received invoices for catering done for social events such as weddings, anniversaries, and parties. When the clients were asked by the caterer to document the payments, most were able to present cancelled checks or other evidence that payments were made for their individual functions. The method of theft was easy. During the meeting with the clients after they had agreed on what the client wanted in the way of services, there would be a down payment to be made. The employee would ask for the down payment to be made payable to him, under the guise that it would speed things along. The employee would cash the check himself, and show the account as still requiring a down payment. If the *office after a period of time asked for payment, the salesman would provide a credit card and account number from another client's account to pay for the account that was being questioned.*

This employee also did this with liquor bills for the functions. He would ask clients if they wanted the caterer to provide liquor for the affair. If the client said yes, the employee advised that he had a market for liquor that would cost the client less than if they went through the caterer. By the client paying him he would save them money. Even when the clients paid the employee, he still submitted the contract showing the caterer supplying the beverages. Thus after the affair was over, the caterer would bill the client for services, to include liquor; all along the client thought he or she had already paid for it.

A similar type of theft can occur when a repair/ serviceman is sent out to repair an appliance, television or some other item. If the customer pays in cash, the serviceman returns to the office and advises that the person had declined service or had someone else fix it. The ticket is voided and the employee pockets the money.

TYPES OF CONTROLS:

"Separation of duties" is a control that should have been in place with the liquor salesman. Only in rare cases should the salesman take the order and deliver the product. If this is your company's procedure and you choose to keep it, then you must install another control to prevent what happened in the above example to your company. Depending on your business that control could be:

- **Return phone call confirming delivery**.
- **Fax to or from the client verifying sale and delivery**.

You should also reduce to writing, a time limit for clients to contact you concerning shortages or other problems with sales or billings.

As to the loss of service as in a caterer, you need two controls:
"Written procedures for your account representatives" so they know what they can and can not do when negotiating a contract with a client. If the employees violate those written and signed instructions you have grounds to dismiss them.

"Call backs to the clients, verifying what they signed and payments made" The account representative has to turn in the paperwork so a client's contract can be scheduled. You need to have someone call the client to confirm what was agreed to. If your account representatives know that the clients are going to receive a call back, they will be less inclined to steal from you using this method.

TYPES OF BUSINESS:

- **COMPANIES WHERE PRODUCT IS DELIVERED BY SALESMAN OR ACCOUNT REPS.**
- **COMPANIES THAT PROVIDE A SERVICE AND RELY ON ACCOUNT REPS. TO MARKET AND NEGOTIATE THOSE SERVICES.**

Theft by inside personnel, technicians or salesmen:

This is a very common form of theft. My experience runs from the bartender that gives out too many "free drinks", to the contractor who loses tools and equipment from the storage or work trailer, through the car dealer that has losses from the counter clerk, up to the employee that steals expensive bank or hospital equipment. These losses range in quantity from a single item to individual thefts that go on for years and require reams of paperwork to document.

This is also the type of theft where the employer stands the worst chance of collecting all that they believe was stolen. You recall the **"exclusion for inventory shortage"** discussed in the chapter on coverage. This is most likely where inventory shortage will show up. Not so much for the single piece of equipment, or list of tools stolen from the work trailer, since the insured should be able to provide invoices for those cases, but in theft of stock, where inventory count is done annually or sometimes not at all. The thefts can go on forever and it is very difficult for the insured to document all they feel they have lost.

> **CASE HISTORY:** *A truck dealership's manager was called by a customer advising the manager that one of the customer's employees had been able to purchase truck parts at a very good discount, first asking for one of two counter persons by name, and then paying cash for the part. The manager contacted the local police authority and a "sting operation" was set up. By this method the theft was uncovered.*
>
> *How the theft was done was not difficult to understand. If you have ever been to an auto or truck parts store or the counter of a dealership where you order parts for your vehicle, you know how the area is set up. For those who have not ordered parts, you normally walk into a room with a long counter. There may be anywhere from one to three counter salespersons there to assist you. Depending on the type store and its age, you may see some of the inventory behind the counter men, or it is behind a wall of the room you are in. You explain what part you want. If it is "in stock" it is obtained by the counter man, an invoice or ticket is written up, the price of the part is obtained from the parts book or computer price list and you pay for the part. Sometimes the ticket is run through the register as it is written up, and at the end of the transaction you receive the part, a copy of the ticket and a receipt for the sale.*
>
> *What the two employees did in this case was run two separate schemes. The first involved regular customers who paid cash and did not ask for a receipt. The employees would hit the* **"no sale"** *button on the register, put the money into the register, and give the customer the change. If the customer did not ask for a receipt the employees would go back into the register at a later time and take out the amount of the purchase. The end result is the employer has lost the amount they paid for that part, plus any profit that would have gone to the company for that sale.*
>
> *The second plan involved a select group of customers that knew if they paid cash they could buy parts at substantial discounts. Again no record of the sale was made. The employees kept the money. The "customer" got a new part for a substantial discount and the company again lost the sale and profit. One ex-*

ample of a sale was a customer that needed a new engine that would normally cost $1,000, but could be bought for cash for $500. Quite a savings.

　　The insured tried to verify their loss by conducting a complete physical inventory and comparing that to what the computer said should be the inventory. On the day the inventory was done the difference was negative $27,000. Based on this and the fact that the sting operation resulted in an arrest, the insured made claim for that amount. However, one employee claimed to have stolen only $1500. The other employee denied any theft. The States Attorney tried to get one employee to turn states evidence on the other, but the end result was that only one was found guilty and received a suspended sentence and probation. There was no apparent restitution to the employer.

From a claim standpoint, the insured was never able to obtain enough documents to confirm a loss close to what they had claimed. When I was instructed to close my file, no payment had been made.

CASE HISTORY: *A car and home stereo and electronics retailer claimed that one of his installers was selling stock **"out the back door"**. The procedure when receiving stock was to log it into the computer system, showing the date it was received, the item ID#, the store stock #, and the cost of the item. When a product was sold, the computer system should not only record the sale but take it off inventory. The loss came to the attention of the owner when someone called and advised that he had purchased a car stereo from an employee without going through regular sales. An investigation was conducted, but the employee was asked to leave with no confession taken and at the time no police involvement.*

　　The insured only had verification of one illegal transaction. But, when he ran his "exception report" he found over $5000 of inventory not accounted for. Did the employee steal that much? He was an installer and had access to inventory, but does one loss worth about $200 open the door for payment of $5000 or more? There was no confession, the police spoke to the individ-

*ual and he confessed to the one theft, but to no more. The em-
ployee never cooperated with me.*

Here are some questions that run through the minds of those
that work in investigating or paying this type of claim.

- Are the "exception report" figures correct. Could the insured
  play with the report to reflect a loss larger than what really
  took place. If there is no illegal action on the part of the insured, and there usually isn't, what else could account for the
  difference between what the report showed and what the
  thief claims he or she stole.
- Was the stock recorded accurately when received? Meaning,
  did they record five stereos when four came in.
- Were sales recorded correctly?
- Who else had access to the stock? Is it possible that some loss
  of inventory was from customers, or taken by other vendors
  when they delivered merchandise for the stereo retailer.
- Is there a second thief? If so you have a second loss and another deductible.

During my investigation I learned that the employer had moved
from one location to another **before** the theft was discovered. Did
any inventory get lost or stolen during the move?. Unfortunately, no
physical inventory was taken after the move.

The only way to confirm the inventory, would have been to conduct a full physical inventory. Depending on the type of inventory
records kept by the insured would determine how difficult it would
be to verify the inventory. If the insured used a **"perpetual inventory
system"** for all inventory it would be fairly easy to determine what the
records indicated should be on hand. In a "perpetual inventory system" there is a record kept for each inventory item, such as 32" television sets. As additional stock in that item is received, the number of
"units" is recorded. As a sale is made, the number of "units" sold is
deducted from the record. This system works well with the advent of
computer software systems available for retailers. The difference be-

tween what this method totals for that "item" versus the actual physical count of that "item" is most likely as a result of "shrinkage", or employee theft. "Perpetual inventory systems" work better in high end retailers, such as Auto dealers, Computer stores, etc.

An inventory audit could also be taken by recording the last physical inventory, add all purchases as of a specific date, and deduct sale of inventory items as of the same date. By conducting another physical inventory using the same date, any difference would be as a result of theft or shrinkage. These audits are expensive. In the above case, the bonding company would have spent almost as much on the audit as they would on the claim. Because of all this, a compromise settlement was made, even though the bonding company knew that they would never be able to collect through subrogation what they paid their insured.

CASE HISTORY: A retail grocer noticed that the cost of goods in the meat department in one of their stores was higher than the other store. Since management bought the same quality of meat for all stores, with pricing being the same, the cost of the goods should also be the same. Since it was higher they knew there was a problem but did not know what it was.

Upper management hired a meat specialist to track sales, but still could not find the problem. However, one day the manager of the store received a telephone call that the manager in the meat department was stealing meat. The store manager decided to check on the manager's actions more closely. One day she saw him leaving the rear of the store through the emergency exit, and he was pushing a shopping cart full of something. She followed at a safe distance and eventually went up to the manager's vehicle which he had parked in the alley way behind the store. He was loading the trunk of his car with meat he had in the shopping cart. The store cost of the meat came to about $1000.

When the meat manager was confronted, he admitted what he was doing. The meat manager was terminated at that point. The police were notified and the meat manager was arrested.

The employee's method was quite simple. Meat was no longer shipped in full sides of beef like it was years ago. Still, meat was received in quantities that required it to be cut down, trimmed and repackaged for sale. The manager would cut the meat for better packaging, but take some of it and place it in his car. He apparently sold it to local restaurants.

The employee did not admit to any sizable theft, yet the profits for the meat department were down significantly. In order to verify or refute the claim, a CPA firm was hired to go over the financial statements for the store in question and compare it to other fiscal years. The auditor's review showed that the gross profit for meat at last year's end was just under 19%. For April the profit was 15.4%, for the months of May and June the profits were a negative 3.1%. Projecting a gross profit similar to April's, would result in a profit of over $22,000. Thus it was the auditor's conclusion that in just two months the store lost over $22,000 in meat. A payment was made for that amount.

The following two examples were considered under crime coverage because the insureds could not prove employee theft, but could prove that a loss occurred. Fortunately for one of the insureds, they had both coverages. (If you recall in an earlier chapter on coverage I wrote that you should have your Employee Dishonesty and other Crime coverage with the same insurance company). The other did not. I want to include these two examples because they probably were thefts from employee dishonesty, and I think the reader can learn from other's errors and lack of controls.

CASE HISTORY: A suburban hospital made claim for theft of surgical equipment. The facts were that the hospital kept equipment and supplies used in surgery in a room located on the surgical floor. When a specific piece of equipment was needed for surgery, a surgical nurse was sent to the room to retrieve it. Upon checking the room, the item was not there.

In my investigation, I found a large room that was used to store everything used in surgery. The room had no full time guard or security camera. The room was locked with a push lock, not a dead bolt. Anyone with a flat object, perhaps even a credit card, could enter the room. Once inside they could take most what they wanted, put it in a bag and walk away. No one would suspect anything. This area was used primarily for employees, but there were construction people working in the vicinity, plus cleaning people at night. There were many exit doors, most did not have panic door or alarms attached. There wasn't enough information to limit this to employee theft. However, the insured was able to confirm purchase of the unit, it could not be located, and a police report was filed. Based on this the claim was paid.

This same insured submitted another similar claim for a different piece of equipment several months later. Again the facts were the same and a claim made. My thoughts were that someone was stealing hospital equipment and either selling it on the street or furnishing a new orthopedics office.

CASE HISTORY: In an earlier chapter I wrote about the regional bank that had a computer called a *"sniffer"* stolen from the room where it and other similar pieces of equipment were stored. The details revealed that the storage room was on the fifth floor in a location that usually only employees would frequent. The door was metal with only a push lock for security. The sign up sheet was not well supervised, but one supervisor was to control the use of this piece of equipment. However, when the computer was discovered missing, the employee that last had it, said that he had returned it. I interviewed other employees that recall using the computer and letting others use it as well. This computer could fit into a large legal briefcase, the type attorneys with many cases in one day would use. There was no search of bags as employees leave the building. There was no inventory alarm placed on the piece itself. The insured felt that the employee that last used it was probably responsible for it's theft, but the police did not think so, and the employee did not admit to any theft.

When considering the poor door lock, the fact that there was loose security with the use of the equipment, and due to others (vendors and cleaning personnel) having access to the area and room where the unit was stored, I could not recommend employee theft to the insurance company. I suggested that since the

⌐ ₌led a police report, and could substantiate the pur-
⌐₋₁ase of this $35,000 plus computer, that a claim be filed under
the crime coverage. Unfortunately, the insured did not have that
coverage. Therefore no payment was made.

TYPES OF CONTROLS:

Concerning loss of inventory from employees that work inside, most controls are either difficult to police or expensive. Since most companies, retail establishments or institutions that have to take inventory have it done once a year, a theft that begins shortly after the last inventory could go on for many months before the next physical inventory reflects a problem. Even then, if you use inventory shortage as your only record of a theft, you probably will have your claim denied. More frequent inventory record taking is costly and causes a loss of sales, or time taken away from productivity. Security guards either add to your payroll or create a substantial outside expense for the company. Of course these two options have to be considered. Here are some less costly controls that may provide what you need:

- **"Signs that remind customers to ask for a receipt"** should be present in any retail store or shop. They should be placed at the cash registers, in plan sight.
- **"Written instructions for employees"** on how a sale is to be completed. If there is a pattern of an employee not following those procedures, he or she will be warned, "in writing", and if it continues, "terminated".
- **"Register tapes should be totaled out each shift"**. By doing this you can review sales, voids, and no-sale openings of the register for that particular work time, and compare them to other employees or time slots. (This is called an **"Average check comparison"**).
- **"Employees should have their own PIN number or access code to the register"**. Also, any sales transaction should include the employee's name or initials. As part of the written

instructions on procedures for sales, employees should not give out their code to another employee for any reason.

- **"Change employee PIN or access numbers on a quarterly basis"** By doing this you minimize the extent of loss, if one employee manages to steal another's code and uses that code to access the registers.
- **"Check register tapes"** should be done by management in order to look for voids, returns or no sales. If there are more of these than the norm for your business, there could be a problem.
- **"Only managers should be allowed to ring up voids, sales or refunds"**. By limiting this to managers you reduce the number of employees that could steal from you using this approach. However, you still must check the work of your manager. As I have shown, managers are also subject to employee dishonesty.
- **"Perform a spot inventory on a specific stock or line of inventory"**. By checking the inventory on a certain style of clothes, or type of auto part or whatever makes up your inventory, you may find out if there an unexplained shortage. I state this because this type of thief usually steals a wide range of inventory. This is done so one supply does not dwindle down faster than normal, thus drawing attention to himself or his department. If your spot inventory shows an unexplained shortage in that group you may have a problem.
- **"Use clear trash bags for removal of trash from the store"**. When employees take the trash out, it is not difficult for them to place smaller inventory in the bag and take it to an accomplice on the outside. There are many inventory items, big in cost, but small enough to fit into a trash bag. Some examples are: car parts, inline skates, lap top computers. By requiring your stores to use clear bags, you reduce the chance of someone placing an item in a trash bag and trying to leave through the rear door.

In companies where inventory can leave through the back door, there are several controls that can help reduce or stop employee theft:

- **"Limit access or control of the rear door"**. In some buildings the rear door is a means to exit as well. Therefore the door or doors cannot be blocked in any way. You should install **"panic type doors"** that will sound an alarm if it is opened. Any key needed to shut off the alarm, in order to receive supplies, stock or even take out the trash, should be held by upper management.
- **"Store management should be there when inventory arrives"**. All inventory should be counted by two people, one of which is at least a store manager.
- **"Make certain the bill of lading matches the physical count"**. This is more for a concern of theft by a delivery person rather than from the employees of the store. However, since there are deliveries made by employees of the company, this control should still be used.

    "Compare sales and cost of goods today versus previous sales periods" This control applies to any company or business that has an inventory. You have to keep good sales records and compare your cost of goods sold to your sales. You cannot afford to do this only yearly. Too much can happen in a year. A bartender can be giving out free drinks to friends, making drinks heavier than he should, or not ringing up all sales. Here is an example: If a bartender misses a sale, pours a heavy drink or gives a drink to friends for a total (all three combined) "loss" of $5.00 per hour, here are the results over a year's time. Assuming two eight hour shifts, that totals to $80 per day. If a bar is open seven days a week, the total is $560 per week. Over a year the grand total $29,120.

    A large retailer with stock in storage must perform test to compare records from one period to another. If there are major differences there could be a problem. You should work with your accountant or CPA to find the best system for your business.

- **"Transfer employees"** In situations where management realizes there is a problem but does not know who it is, they should consider transfers. By doing this, if theft was going on, this will end the problem in the section or department that you were concerned about. If a problem begins in another department, it is possible that your concerns have moved from one section to the other. You should be able to focus on the person that you transferred until you catch him.

Companies that have inventory being shipped out from a warehouse or wholesale storage area have several controls as well that can have an effect on theft.

- **"Separation of duties:** refers to the delivery person not being the same person that fills the order.
- **"Supervisory check off of inventory from storage to delivery vehicle".** The bill of lading should match what is being loaded. Someone in management should do this, on an occasional and unscheduled basis in order to rule out any long term theft.

Companies that have inventory, e.g. retail stereo or computer store, or equipment, e.g. bank, hospital, that is kept in a back room or specific storage area need the following:

- **"Store equipment or inventory in a secure room"** This means a dead bolt lock or combination lock with only a few people with the key or combination to that lock.
- **"Written check-out sheet for inventory"** Make sure the employees know that they are responsible for that equipment until it is signed back in. I realize you cannot have this done on every piece of inventory, but it certainly can be used for your higher priced pieces of equipment or your more popular inventory items. If it is an installer who is going to install equipment in a customer's vehicle, whomever controls the inventory access should "require a sales ticket or sales number" before giving out the item.

Certain companies have open or visible inventory to the public as well as to the employees. Most of the above controls apply to this group of employers as well: however, **"security cameras"** if used properly, are an excellent means of additional control. I will discuss them in the chapter 12.

TYPES OF BUSINESS:

- COMPANIES THAT SELL PARTS, OR SUPPLIES FOR VEHICLES, APPLIANCES, HOME FURNISHINGS, CONSTRUCTION TOOLS AND EQUIPMENT.

- MANUFACTURING FACILITIES THAT SHIP THEIR PRODUCTS TO RETAILERS OR TO THE CONSUMER DIRECTLY.

- COMPANIES THAT SELL RETAIL ITEMS; COMPUTERS, STEREOS, EXPENSIVE JACKETS, SPORT EQUIPMENT, SHOES.

- COMPANIES THAT SELL FOOD OR DRINK; GROCERS, LIQUOR STORES, BARS AND CLUBS.

- INSTITUTIONS THAT USE EXPENSIVE AND EASILY CARRIED OFF EQUIPMENT OR INVENTORY FOR DAILY OPERATIONS; PHOTOGRAPHIC STUDIOS, CONSTRUCTION OFFICES, DOCTOR'S OFFICES, BANKS, MEDICAL FACILITIES.

Chapter Eleven

Methods of Theft
and
Management Controls
(After hiring)

Cash, Deposits, Revenue, Premiums

I have separated the theft of cash and deposits from the other methods of theft for several reasons. As you probably know, in any employee theft, cash money is the bottom line. However, in the methods discussed in the last chapter there was always an extra step before the theft turned into money. If it was theft by fraudulent invoice, the invoice had to be typed, perhaps a fake supporting paper authored, the invoice sent to accounting, a check cut and that check would have to be negotiated. If it was theft of a check, it had to be stolen or forged, and then negotiated. In the theft of cash, deposits or revenues, methods used usually result in a direct collection of usable cash or money by the thief.

Additionally, there are many ways that theft of cash is done, with the methods used sometimes requiring a separate set of controls to minimize that theft. Finally, since some employers are concerned with only the potential of theft or loss of cash, by having a separate chapter it makes it easier for the reader to find the area they need to review.

THEFT OF CASH FROM CASH REGISTERS:

There is a fine difference between this discussion and the theft of inventory using cash register activity that was discussed in the last chapter. These examples of theft are not only informative, but reveal how easy it is to steal cash. By reading these examples the reader can identify areas that may be weak in his own company.

CASE HISTORY: An auto dealership claimed that a parts manager had become involved in theft of money by voiding transactions and by removing copies of parts invoices from the receipt book.

This was a very tedious loss to investigate for many reasons. First, the theft was going on for many years, and so much time had gone by before any loss was suspected. The paper trail was long, yet not always indicative of a loss. That means there were signs of improper record keeping, yet that did not always mean employee theft had occurred. Second, there was more than one method of theft used, which made for a more complicated auditing process. Third, the insured felt that since a loss had taken place, their loss of sales, in comparison to other months was indicative of a theft of more than the available investigation and records showed. This caused some tension between the insured and his agent on one side and the bonding company on the other, with myself in the middle fielding calls from both sides.

Here is the background. Normally a manager of the parts department should not be the one that has daily contact with customers. His or her job is to supervise the department, handle complaints, paperwork etc. The dealership was on a computer system for recording sales of parts. Sometimes the computer would be down for whatever reason and when that occurred, there was a manual parts invoice book, with ascending numbering on each invoice.

There were several copies of each manual invoice, one for the customer, one for the parts department, and one for the main office. There were four computer invoices for each sale, an original went to the accounting department, and one copy each for parts, front office and the customer.

The dealership learned over a year before the loss was discovered that they were losing manual invoices. This means that many invoices were not coming into the office. They did not know where the loss was from, nor did management know that a loss of an invoice meant a theft. They asked the parts manager to look into it but after several more months nothing was discovered.

A private investigator was retained, but he was not able to pinpoint theft. However, one day, someone from management went into the parts department and counted the sales, by invoice number. When the sales were totaled in accounting later in the day, there were less sales than when they had been counted by the person from management. Therefore, they knew the theft was coming from the person that was counting the invoices and submitting them. That person was the manager. He was interviewed, verbally gave some indication that he had stolen and was terminated. There was no written confession and no police involvement. In his interview with me he denied any theft from the dealership.

*Records reflected a large number of missing manual invoices, but there was a question if every missing invoice constituted a loss. It was my thinking that if an invoice was removed from the book, that it was probably done by someone in the parts department in order to hide some illegal activity. After an unofficial audit, I made a recommendation to the bonding company for payment. This **would** have been paid by the insurance company, except a second method of theft caused a problem in concluding the loss in its entirety.*

*The second method used was to **void** or **credit** computer sales after they were completed. This was done in the computer itself. By doing this there would be no record of the sale. The amount of the sale could then be removed from the register.*

*The parts manager had the time to perform these thefts. Since it was not unusual for him to be at the register no one thought anything odd of his **working** there. Additionally, because he had computer access, he was able to work with the records and turn many transactions from a sale to a **void** or **credit** and then cash to himself.*

In trying to verify whether a customer was granted a refund for a sale, sometimes the only way was to contact the customer directly. In most cases so much time had passed from the date of the sale to the date of discovery and our investigation, that the customer's records were either in storage or no longer available. In some cases, the customers did tell me that they remembered the transactions and that there were no refunds or return of goods. In a review of past computer print outs, there were examples of these **voids** *or* **refunds** *appearing in the computer records going back several years. The question arose, did those few cases where the customers responses indicated theft, represent that all of the voids or refunds appearing in the computer printouts were thefts. Since there was no confession, initially the bonding company took the position that the insured had to prove that they* **were** *all thefts before they would make any payments. I was asked to close my file because the bonding company felt that additional investigation would not turn up any more information.*

At the time of my file closing, no payments had been made to the insured. Recently, I spoke to the general manager of the dealership. He advised that they received nearly a $100,000 from the insurance company. As I review the file, the only way the loss could have been that large was for the company to accept that the **voids** *and* **refunds** *in the computer printouts were a fair representation of the theft.*

With all the copies of sales going to several departments, one would think that the loss would have been discovered earlier, but the staff that reads those records has to know what the readings actually mean in order to discover that there is a possible problem. **Education of your employees is essential to good prevention.**

As to the employee, the dealership never pressed charges against him. I was told that he is working in the area, perhaps for another car dealership.

CASE HISTORY: *A retail clothing store with several locations discovered that one of their stores had a large number of* **voids** *transactions as compared to other stores for the same period of time. Here are some figures: in a six month period, one store had* **voids** *totaling over $40,000, which compared to* **voids** *of $14,000 from all other stores combined for the same period. In one month, this store had over a 130* **voids** *compared to 7 or 10* **voids** *in other stores. The insured hired a consultant to audit the* *records for this period of time. This required review of all transactions of all stores to make sure that a comparison could be made and the same testing applied.*

The cash register used in this store would provide a receipt that gave the time that the sale was made, along with all sales information. The theft took place by an employee going back into a sale by cash transaction, voiding the sale and removing the cash from that sale. When a **void** *is done the register issues the same type of receipt as the sale except the word* **"void"** *appears on the receipt. The receipt of the sale and* **void** *is also recorded on the cash register tape. This is a continuous tape for that shift or that day. By reviewing the tape, the accountant was able to find all* **voids** *and check them against the sales information. The time of sale was recorded along with the salesperson that made the sale.*

When the consultant reviewed the register tape, she checked the location of the **voids** *in relation to the last transaction before it, and after it. By checking the time recorded from those transactions she concluded, correctly, that the* **void** *took place between those two times. In comparing the time of sale versus the time of the* **void** *there would usually be several hours between the two.*

The cash register system also recorded the employee number used by the person recording the **void**. *In review of the sales records the majority of* **voids** *were recorded by the same two employee numbers. Since the register required employees to use their own PIN number to gain access to the register it is unlikely that someone else was using another employee's PIN.*

You may be saying to yourself that these **voids** by themselves do not indicate a theft. That is a correct assessment. Furthermore, in most cases there was no customer name found on the receipt, making it very difficult to prove theft. The insurance company could have rejected the information as not being sufficient to indicate theft, however, in all reality how many **voids** are considered average for this type of store. When you see the wide disparity in numbers of **voids** between this one store and the others, any accounting professional would realize that there was some theft taking place.

In this situation the insured did not have very much coverage. In fact the loss from one month exceeded the amount of coverage that was in force at the time the loss was discovered. Based on the overwhelming documentation, it was the position of the insurance company to pay the claim without requiring additional proof by the insured. As it was, the insured spent several thousand dollars auditing the stores records to this point. It would have been unproductive to document more. Now, if the insured had larger limits, say $100,000, more proof would have been required.

As to the employees involved, both were terminated without providing any confessions. As of this writing, the States Attorney has been given over six boxes of documentation but has not issued any indictments.

CASE HISTORY: *I investigated the theft of money from a large truck stop location. Besides serving the trucks themselves, there was a 24 hour restaurant on the premises. The company had installed a cash register software system that was to total all sales for the shifts. There were two registers for each shift, except the early morning shift which required one register. One day, one of the employees saw another employee emptying a lot of paper in the dumpster. The employee told the manager, who in turn decided to inspect the dumpster. He found several days daily report papers for the morning shift.*

*The manager did some checking of the sales figures and found that the software system was not picking up any sales for the morning shifts. However, the daily register tape **did** show that there were sales for that shift. To put this in dollar terms, the total daily reports would total for example $2700. When the manager totaled the sales based on the register tape the total might be $3300. Bob, the manager found out that the early morning shift was always the one missing.*

When the employee that was seen throwing the papers away was confronted, she admitted to theft, but only $600. Her method was very interesting. She found out that if she entered an incorrect date prior to calling up the totals of the shift, the computer erased the totals of that shift. Fortunately, as I explained *above, the computer did not erase the sales record of that shift from the detail tape. This is how the insured was able to verify the loss.*

The loss information was given to me in seven large boxes. I did a random sampling using the 80/20 rule. This means you verify twenty percent of the loss to infer that 80 percent of the claim is valid. Prior to being directed to close my file, I had met with the employee's attorney. The employee was married with a family and stole because of financial problems. The employee had spent the $70,000 she stole in over nine months.

In speaking with the manager of the truck stop, I was advised that the employee pled guilty, was prosecuted and given a short jail sentence. She is currently on work release, and is slowly paying back what was stolen.

CASE HISTORY: *The office manager for a small dental group stole money by not recording into the system sales that were paid in cash. Most of the patients had dental insurance or paid by check. However, there were some patients that paid in cash. Some did not ask for a receipt.*

*The office manager would take the money from the patient, ring up a **no sale** on the register and place the funds inside. Later in the day she would withdraw those transactions that were cash and where no receipt was given.*

This theft went on for many months before the dentist found that patients he remembered seeing were not listed as having been seen. By contacting a few patients the loss was discovered. The loss was not very large, only about $5,000.

The manager confessed to the theft and a promissory note was signed where she agreed to pay back to the bonding company, over time, the amount she stole. The insured did not want to prosecute and draw embarrassment to the group.

CASE HISTORY: *A large volume liquor store owner was reviewing security camera video tapes of his cashiers when he noticed that there was an indication that employees were not requiring* certain customers to pay for the liquor they were buying. The owner also noticed what appeared to be employees hitting the **no sale** button on the register, and giving some change to the customer for what was purchased.

The insurance company asked me to review all the video tapes and then conduct an investigation. In reviewing the tapes, it was clear that employees were giving away stock to certain buyers, and that they were opening the register using the **no sale** button. But, I did not see any employees go into the register and remove funds and put it in their pocket.

The owners had four employees sign confessions for about $1,000 each. Three of the employees would not cooperate with me, but one did. In his statement he confessed to giving liquor away at a discounted amount. He denied taking any money himself, yet he signed a confession for $1,000. He told me he signed it because they would have prosecuted him if he didn't.

After the insureds reviewed their profit and loss statements, they found that the cost of goods was very high and profits for the last two years were extremely low as compared to the other years. Based on that, the insured felt that the loss was over $300,000. This loss occurred nearly ten years ago. The annual sales of the company at the time were over three million. The insureds asked for a settlement of $100,000 based on four separate employees stealing individually. An audit satisfied the insurance company that a loss of at least $100,000 was possible. In review of the video tapes the employees worked so closely together that each had to know what the others were doing. In the statement of the employee that spoke to me, he admitted that others were involved but he would not give me names or details.

Based on the above information, the insurance company had to decide if there was evidence that the four employees were working together. If so, the maximum payment would be the policy limit of $25,000. But if the company could not prove collusion, then the loss would be $100,000. Four different employees working separately would be four different losses for a total exposure of $100,000. My initial authority was $50,000, the insured wanted more than that. Eventually the loss settled in the area of $60,000.

TYPE OF CONTROLS:

Controls for cash register or money drawer losses can be simple or they can be complicated, depending on a number of factors such as the size of the company, how many stores or offices, number of employees, and the type sales and exposures the company has. Most companies should design their controls in accordance with the amount of information that the sales system provides and who is going to read and interpret that data.

"Upper management must check for 'voids,'refunds' and 'no sales' on the register tapes". This is the most important control. Anyone that has cash transactions that involve the use of a cash register must understand that in almost every case of theft, money first goes in the register and then it is taken out by the thief. Since the amount of money in the register or "till" is supposed to balance out in accordance with sales for that day, the thief must do something to insure that the drawer balances out.

If the employee is taking cash from the "customer" or "patient" and not ringing it up, he or she must hit the **no sale** button on the register to open it, put the money on the register, give the customer or patient change and then put the money into the register. The register tape is not going to record the sale, so the register is over by the net amount of the transaction.

If the employee is taking cash from the customer, ringing it up as a valid sale and giving them a copy of the receipt issued from the register, the employee has to create a **void** or **refund** or **delete** transaction so he or she can remove the net amount of that sale from the register.

" Zee out the register tape every shift" This way if there is a shortage you will know who was working that shift. This would help in narrowing down the employee responsible. ("Zee out"is a retail term that refers to totaling the sales for a shift, or a day, on the cash register tape. After the tape is "Zeed out, the sales start over from zero again.)

"Written procedure for 'voids', 'refunds', etc." Only management should do **voids**. All employees should read and sign acknowledgement of these procedures. Management should have in their job description to check all register tapes for **voids** at the end of the day. Any unusual numbers should be reported to upper management.

"**Upper management must check the work of store or shop managers**" Because people in charge or in management also become thieves, as in the case of the manager of the parts department, upper management must have its own written procedures for people in the office of management to follow. This is necessary to check on the accuracy of the people in charge of the various departments. In the case of the car dealer, there were computer printouts that were showing the word **void** or **refund** on a large number of transactions. Someone should have picked that up and investigated.

"**Manager's procedures for supervision of daily sales**" In the case of the employee that stole from the truck stop, management should have been checking for the paperwork on all five shifts. It is hard to believe that they would let this go for so long. There should have been written instructions for the manager to follow, with upper management checking on the manager's work. The manager could have on at least a weekly basis, compared the daily reports to the cash register tapes. Had he done so, the loss would have been several hundred not thousands of dollars. The sales figures were sent to the home office in another state. Someone in the home office should have been aware of the number of registers and the number of shifts, and should have made inquires into the situation there. Obviously, either upper management had not explained to the store manager his responsibilities, or someone wasn't doing their job effectively. Just think what would have happened if the manager, had been in collusion with the employee, the loss may have gone on for years.

TYPES OF BUSINESS:

- **ALL RETAIL STORES AND SHOPPES,**

- **COMPANIES THAT SELL A PRODUCT OVER THE COUNTER,**

- **RESTAURANTS, BARS, LOUNGES, LIQUOR STORES, DRY CLEANERS**

- **PROFESSIONAL PRACTICES,**

- **FEDERAL BANKS, AND SAVINGS AND LOAN INSTITU-TIONS**

THEFT OF CASH DEPOSITS AND SALES:

Regarding the theft of deposits, this theft usually occurs when the employee removes cash from a deposit that is to go to the bank for the company or business where the employee works. Normally the entire deposit is not taken because that would be difficult to hide. What usually occurs is the employee removes some or all of the cash from a deposit, holds the deposit until other checks are received, then puts those checks with the first deposit to cover the cash that was taken from the first deposit. This is known as **"rolling the deposit"**.

CASE HISTORY: The treasurer of a hospital auxiliary called the finance office to report that she noticed deposits were being posted in the bank very late in relation to when they were given to the cashier of the hospital for deposit. The hospital finance officer reviewed several bank statements and compared them to copies of deposit records sent to the finance office and discovered that there was a significant time lag between the copy of the deposit being sent to the finance office and to the bank.

The hospital cashiers had the responsibility of working with money from several departments of the hospital. The cashiers were to total all deposits on a daily basis, send a copy of the deposit to finance, and the original to the bank.

When the finance officer approached the cashiers, one of them admitted to theft. What she admitted doing was taking the cash from whatever source that brought the cash into the cashier's office, substituting other checks for that cash and making up the deposits. The cashier had to send the copies to finance on a daily basis otherwise she would have been caught sooner.

The employee kept copies of the deposits that were to go to the bank. The record of "lagging deposits" went back three *years. That would normally result in a five figure loss, but in these type of thefts you are constantly using today's money to complete yesterday's deposit, so the actual amount stolen is minimal for any given day. The employee may have diverted or delayed over $50,000 in deposits but the actual loss was under $10,000. The cashier confessed to the amount of theft. She had gotten into financial difficulties from some marital problems. According to the insured, the employee admitted to theft, was prosecuted, found guilty, given a sentence with most or all time suspended, given community service hours and the requirement to provide restitution to the hospital.*

CASE HISTORY: *The manager of a corporation that offered arcade type games for adults confessed to stealing deposits to support his gambling habit. The accountants of the company had been asking for the financial records from the manager for many months. The manager was able to stall the accountants. Finally, one of the accountants notified the president of the corporation and a meeting was called. In that meeting the manager confessed his theft.*

The manager, Barry, was very cooperative. He supplied a statement summarizing that he would take in monies from the operation of the business, hold the deposits until he had enough checks to cover the cash he had taken out, and then make a deposit. When Barry confessed, he made available envelopes that he had marked with the amounts that the deposits should have been. This shows that he had every intention to pay back what he had stolen, but was not able to.

The loss went on for about two years. Sometimes the deposits would be received in the bank thirty days or more from the date that was written on the deposit. Barry admitted adding checks to the deposits that were dated after the date on the deposit slip itself. Yet there is no indication that anyone noticed any of this or made any inquires until the time that the loss was discovered.

The loss was over $70,000, however the settlement was a compromise, in the area of $15,000, due to a strong possibility that there was no coverage for the theft. Barry was not paid as an *employee. Since he was a director of the company, and its for-mer president, he could have been excluded from coverage. However, he was functioning as an employee when he made up and deposited money received from sales. The investigation did not reveal any audits showing that there were any problems in the business.*

Another method of theft concerns the theft of an entire deposit. I have had employees say they were robbed while using a men's room and the deposit was taken. I have had the managers of fast food chains, and pizza parlors complete the deposit from the previous days sales, place it down on the desk or counter to field a phone call or answer a complaint, return and find it missing.

These usually total no more than one or two thousand dollars. Sometimes someone confesses, but usually it is difficult to determine who was responsible. Was it one of the employees,or the manager himself? Could a customer somehow have gotten to the money? You do not want to spend a thousand dollars investigating a two thousand dollar loss. The police departments will take a report but not much else, because the loss is small.

As long as the company has full coverage the insurance company will usually make a payment under the other crime coverage.

Sometimes the loss is larger due to an oversight in management allowing more money to be available than there should be. In those situations it is a different ballgame.

CASE HISTORY: A large cinema corporation had experienced a substantial $18,000 theft from one of its multi-theater com-plexes. The procedures required deposits to be made whenever there was more than $2,000 in sales. However, the manager felt that he could make the deposits on Monday for the weekend's business, because he did not have enough deposit bags, and money deposited on Monday would be given credit as if it had been deposited on Saturday.

On the night of the theft the manager, Robert, counted the sales from ticket purchases of Friday and Saturday. After counting the money, he placed the money and deposit slip in a deposit bag and put it in a file cabinet located in the front room of the office, instead of using the safe in the rear office. He set the alarm, and left the office. The security camera and alarm were working. On the way out of the building there was a door alarm that was also set. He was the last one to leave. On Sunday he came to the theaters in early afternoon. Several employees were already there. When he walked into the office he found that the alarm was off, the tape from the security camera had been taken, but more importantly the money was taken from the file cabinet.

The investigation centered around five employees. There were no signs of forced entry, either to the building or to the office. The central station that monitors the alarm verified that the alarm was disarmed early in the night, and that the alarm code used was that of a vice president of the company. Whomever stole the money had to have a key to the front door, know the alarm codes, the PIN of someone that had access, plus know where the money had been placed, then have the experience to find and remove the video tape. The person also must have known that there was a considerable amount of money in the office to make the theft worthwhile.

My investigation determined that management was lax with the keys. Several former employees still had keys to the building. Additionally, the list of PINs was sometimes left out on the desk where anyone in the office, usually people at the management level, could see it. The State Police did an investigation, including polygraph exams. At the end of their investigation the information seemed to point to one person, but at the time of this file being closed no arrest had been made. I have recently spoken to the State Police and a spokesperson advised that they are going to close their investigation with no arrest.

The bonding company made a payment because all signs pointed to employee theft of cash, even though a specific employee could not be identified.

TYPES OF CONTROLS:

"Written instructions on bank deposits" is the first control. This should cover how often they are to be made, by whom and how often they will be checked. Employees should be made aware that any deviation will result in termination. These instructions must be given to the office clerk, bookkeeper or accountant that is to receive the deposit copy so they know how often to expect a deposit and who to report to if the schedule is not followed.

"Testing of one or more deposits by upper management" to see how long it takes the deposit to be posted in the bank. This will tell upper management if there is a possible problem before it becomes large. Upper management should also be aware of the general frequency of deposits, the average amounts, and how those deposits are broken down. If you are used to seeing deposits with cash along with checks and you begin to see deposits that only have checks, or the cash amount is small compared to what it used to be, you may have a problem.

'Two people sign for the deposits" Since it is the function of the cashier or manager of a retail establishment to make up and usually deposit the sales for a given period, it is difficult to have any separation of duties as I have suggested in previous chapters. However, if upper management requires two to sign for the deposit you reduce the chance of having one person do what the cashier did in the hospital case.

"Periodic review of cashier's or manager's efficiency" Even if you have two people sign for the deposits, upper management must still check the work in each department. If this is not done you run the risk of having a substantial loss, because **people in trust have access and opportunity, all they need is motive.**

There are a number of controls such as keys, alarm systems and pass codes that would fit any loss exposure similar to the cinema loss. I will cover those controls in Chapter 12, General Controls. They could apply to many employer situations.

TYPES OF BUSINESS:

- **FAST FOOD STORES, DRY CLEANERS**
- **RETAIL DEPARTMENT STORES**
- **CHECK CASHING STORES**
- **ENTERTAINMENT INDUSTRY (THEATERS, OPERA HOUSES, CONCERT HALLS)**
- **HOSPITALS AND OTHER LARGE MEDICAL FACILITIES**
- **COMPANIES THAT HAVE CASHIER OFFICES**

THEFT OF REVENUE OR DEPOSITS ON PURCHASES:

I find these type losses interesting because they require the customer to be gullible, with little street smarts on how these transactions should be completed. These are cases where a representative of the employer, perhaps a salesman or property manager or account representative, receives cash that the customer thinks is going to go to the sale or contract, but doesn't. Here are two examples.

CASE HISTORY: A car dealer had a used car salesman that collected, as part of his duties in any sale, down payments from customers. He would sometimes not give the customer a receipt, or if they asked for a receipt would give a generic one that did not refer to the deal in question. When the customer went to close the deal, the contract would show the amount of the down payment as not collected. Yet the customer paid the salesman. By the time several deals like this came to the surface, the employee had quit his job as a used car salesman.

In the investigation it was learned that this salesman had a history of doing this. He would stay long enough to make some quick hits, then leave for other employers. Since he left before the losses were discovered it was more difficult to gain the em-

ployee's cooperation. In this case the employee did meet with me, gave a statement refuting the allegations of the customers in the five deals that he was accused of improper handling of funds.

There were some receipts signed by the employee and conversations with the customers that led me to believe that there was theft involved. When I spoke with the police and they advised that they had past dealings with this employee, I recommended that the payments be made. Eventually the employee was found guilty and given probation.

CASE HISTORY: This type of loss is somewhat similar to the account executive for the catering company, but instead of being given checks, he or she is paid in cash. This case involved a real estate company that managed and rented hundreds of properties throughout the city. There were several property managers, each assigned a number of properties. One manager went in business for himself. When he was successful in renting an apartment, he had the tenant sign the appropriate lease and collected the security deposit. He advised the tenants that they were to pay him. If the person paid in cash the manager kept the money. When the tenant paid with a check he told the tenant that the checks could not be negotiated and asked that the tenant obtain a certified check payable to the property manager. This went on for several months.

The theft was discovered when one of the tenants sent their payment to the real estate company directly. When the office clerk found that there was no indication that payments had been received on that property, she went to the property manager who advised that he would take care of it. The incident got back to the owner, who then sent another property manager to the building for an inspection. The second property manager discovered that the property was rented, but no rents had been received from all the tenants in that building.

Eventually the thief confessed, and a payment was made to the insured for their loss, about $8,000. The employee did show a desire to reimburse for what he had stolen. No police were involved.

TYPES OF CONTROLS:

These are tough losses to prevent from occurring. As the employer, you have little control over what your agent or representative is going to say or do with a customer or client until you receive a complaint. Obviously if you receive a number of complaints perhaps you have to consider speaking to the employee, job transfer or termination.

When your employee is in a position to accept monies from your clients you are vulnerable. You cannot be there for every transaction or contract, thus you will not know what **"arrangements"** have been made.

But here are some things that you can do to minimize the theft before it occurs. In the case of a car or truck dealer, retail sales company or insurance agency, real estate office, or any business where customers come into a show room or office, you should:

- **"Have brochures or pamphlets available"** thanking the customer for coming into the store, dealership, insurance or real estate office. This "flyer"should explain the buying process to them. It should also remind the customer to always ask for a receipt and check to make sure the receipt is for the amount of money paid.If your business requires that salesmen or agents greet every potential customer as they walk in, say that in the flyer. Explain in a few words what the salesman's role is and what monies if any they should collect.
- **"Make sure salesman and agents know the correct buying process"** You should make sure that it is followed.
- **"Sign in sheet for Customers"** so your office staff could check back with the customer to see how they were treated and if any purchases were made. If there was a sale your staff could verify the monies paid in that sale.

Concerning someone that goes out to meet a client or prospective tenant, you may not know who they met with and the results of that meeting. You will have to keep a watchful eye on the supplies in your office or procedures that your employee would need to follow in order to complete a theft. It could be a receipt book. Make sure all receipt books are accounted for as well as the individual receipts in each book. This includes receipts in the front and back of the book.

"One person responsible for giving insurance rates", if it is an insurance or warranty policy that could be the source of stolen premium. If that person had to be given the name of the prospective insured, in order to quote a rate, there would be a record of any meeting. The rating supervisor could also have follow up contact with the client to check on their decision or the service that was given to them.

"Periodically check your real estate holdings" in order to compare revenue history of your properties. If someone on your staff is trying to collect rent for themselves, they have to make the books and records look like the property has been rented. But it would be difficult for that person to forge rental income records. It could be done, but that would usually require either two people working together or very poor controls over the accounts receivables. You should also have a good idea how long your properties stay vacant. If one is showing no income for longer than it has in the past, it is worth checking out.

TYPES OF BUSINESS:

- **NEW AND USED AUTO AND TRUCK DEALERS,**
- **HOME IMPROVEMENT, AND GENERAL BUILDING CONTRACTORS,**
- **PLUMBING, ELECTRICAL AND HEATING CONTRACTORS,**
- **INSURANCE AGENCIES AND FINANCIAL INSTITUTIONS,**
- **REAL ESTATE PROPERTY MANAGEMENT FIRMS.**

This concludes the **"methods of theft"** and specific **"management controls"** that I believe would stop those "methods of theft" if they were put in place and consistently reviewed.

The final chapter is a summary of **"General management controls"** and **"Security topics"** that apply to "employee theft", and in some cases to other crimes as well.

Chapter Twelve

General Management Controls
and Other Security Topics

As you can imagine, over the years of investigating employee dishonesty losses, I have been asked my opinion on a number of "management control" subjects as well as "security" issues.

In the previous chapters that discussed management controls, I tried to focus the control on a particular method of theft in connection with a specific industry or exposure. As you read, many controls overlap into many different areas of employment, as do security topics.

In this chapter I will discuss several controls and security measures that for the most part could be used by many employers who are trying to minimize their employee theft losses. Some comments will apply not only to the possibility of employee theft but also to other theft situations that may or may not be at the hands of an employee.

These comments are my own based on years of being in this business, and seeing what does and does not work.

EMPLOYEE/EMPLOYER RELATIONS:

Under this heading there are several areas in the relationship between the employee and employer that refer to employee dishonesty or the possibility of employee dishonesty.

"How much should other employees know about an employee theft"

This was touched on earlier in the text, but it deserves repeating. I do not think it is wise to inform all employees that a certain employee en if you have a confession from the employee and a subsequent conviction, should you choose to prosecute, giving out the employee's name around the office or warehouse is not going to have much of a positive effect on the employees. First, because they probably already heard through the employee grapevine about what happened. Second, if an employee is going to steal from you, their need to steal is going to over shadow their concern about what might happen if they are caught.

CASE HISTORY: *If a cocaine user can steal money from her parents, and leave her children behind because she did not have the physical or mental patience for them, do you think the fear of being caught is going to deter someone that has a great need for money. (This case was discussed in chapter ten, involving the bookkeeper of the contractor).*

Third, your discovery of the theft and subsequent confession or conviction of the employee will cause great embarrassment and problems for the thief:

- He may have family and friends that he will have to face.
- He may need to sell his home.
- He may not find another job.
- He may file for bankruptcy.
- There is the possibility of jail or civil litigation.

There is only so much that a person can take. If the employer adds to that by sharing with other employees the details of the theft and who is responsible, the employee may react against **you**, the employer.

What should be done is make sure that all employees know, from the time you hire them, what your company philosophy is on employee theft. This disclosure should be in writing.

You could hold meetings and take feed back from employees on how they perceive employee theft.

Should you experience a theft, and you know who it is, follow the procedures outlined in this study.

After the theft is over and you have a conviction, I think it is okay to make a general statement to the employees that "you may or may not know that we experienced a theft by one of our employees' (do not mention any names). The person has been convicted. The matter has been concluded (never say what or how much was stolen) and we hope it does not happen again."

"Employee rewards and suggestions"

Several times employers have asked if they should set up some sort of system where employees can collect a reward by telling management about employees that are stealing. I do not like this idea. I have read where this has been suggested by accountants, and other risk professionals. I do not like it because what if one or two people do not like a co-worker and set him or her up to **look** like he or she stole. You could be faced with a lawsuit filed by that employee, if your allegations are found to be false. Even if it is dismissed as a mistake, you will probably lose the good employee to someone else.

What I can suggest is to set a small prize if an employee comes forward with an idea to improve security or cost controls.

You could also allow employees to provide anonymous comments about theft, in writing. You should then consult with a risk consultant, attorney or accountant before taking any further steps. You should not place a reward for doing this memo. I feel it gives the employee the wrong reason to reveal what they think they saw.

"Meetings"

I think it is a good idea to have occasional meetings. It gives the employees a feeling that they belong. This is especially true if the employer asks for comments from the employees on ways that can improve the employees' situation and in turn the company's relationship with the employees. If an employee feels that he or she is an important person in the company's eyes, and or that the company officers care about the employees, they may think twice before engaging in employee theft.

. all meetings should be negative ones either. I see no point in having a positive meeting and end it on a negative note.

On the other hand, if there is a situation where you find that something illegal may be going on, or certain employee behavior is not following company policy, a meeting should be called as soon as practical.

SECURITY METHODS:

"Moles"

These are people you hire to work with employees to try and uncover employee theft. They go through the regular employment process and co-mingle with the employees. These are usually private investigators. I believe this type of control works best in a warehouse, or job site exposure. Any office worker or supervisor that is involved in theft is going to work alone and when no one else is there. Remember, the reference to employees that come in early in the day or work late at night?

If you decide to use a "mole," make sure that you have valid information that you are having a theft problem and where that problem might be. This way you can try and focus your **"mole"** in that direction. Be sure to use a private investigator that is licensed and comes with good recommendations. Also make sure you agree on the fee, and the amount of time you want the investigator to work.

"Surveillance"

This also comes under the control of a PI, or possibly the police department. If the potential loss is big enough you may get the police to do surveillance for you. However, usually you will have to hire someone to conduct observations for you. Again this works better in a retail store warehouse or delivery dock situation, but I have seen it used in liquor stores, retail stores and construction sites.

Just as with the "mole", use the same level of people. Make certain that they carry professional liability insurance coverage and that it is in force.

"Company keys and pass codes"

The biggest problem with keys is that the employer has so many out in use, that if someone with an office key came into the office or building and removed company supplies or equipment, the employer is not going to know who could be responsible. Whenever there are no signs of forced entry, the police and investigators first look to employees that have keys, or to vendors that had access during the off hours, such as a janitorial service.

Obviously, the more keys that are out and in use make it more difficult to try and determine who came into the building. An employee who wants to make a few extra dollars by entering the office and removing equipment such as, supplies, laptop computers, and company documents, can do this without much chance of getting caught, assuming that they do not do this every day or every month.

If you as the employer have to keep keys as the only means of entering or leaving the office, here are a few things you can do **"to minimize your exposure"**:

- Only a short list of employees should have keys to the building or office.
- If possible have the key stamped that it cannot be duplicated.
- Whenever an employee leaves, if that employee had a key it should be taken back.
- If you terminate someone and you have a bad feeling about that person you may want to consider changing keys and locks.
- Make sure you keep an up to date list of who has keys.
- If possible consider installation of a security camera, for the entrance, with the video recorder kept in a locked room to which only the employer has access.
- Consider installation of a pass code or card entry system. The card system is great. I will discuss them in the following section.

In many offices keys to the building itself are somewhat passe'. With the advent of pass codes or security cards the security is much better. Here is how they work. Entrance to the building or office can only be made by either pressing a code number in a letter pad on the entrance door, or by sliding a pass card through a slit on the door entrance which allows it to open. The problem with the pass code is that it is not going to identify a specific person. You would only know that someone that had or knew the code came in.

There are more sophisticated pass codes that work with alarm systems. When an employee or vendor enters the building they have so many seconds to put in the alarm code and a PIN number. This PIN number is to be their very own, not shared or available to others. It does not always work that way, but if it did you would know, by the records kept at the alarm company, who came in and at what time.

The pass card system is usually connected to a full time security or central station company just like the alarm system. The only difference is there is no alarm. Most cards are coded in such a way that when the card is pulled along the strip, it sends an electronic message to the central station recording that card number. Since everyone issued a card has a different number, the central station could tell, by reviewing their records, whose card was used, and at what time.

The pass codes should be changed and or the pass cards collected whenever an employee that has one leaves employment.

"Alarm systems"

Adding to what was stated above, there are several types of alarms. The two types that I am the most familiar with are perimeter and motion detectors. There are a large number of alarm companies out there, most will give you a free inspection of your situation. Here are points you should know. The alarm is only as good as the central station that monitors it. Make sure that you know how many calls the central station makes before they call the police. For example, I just completed a security and employee theft survey for an art dealer. The owner explained that they had an alarm company with a monitoring station. If an alarm sounded in the studio, the monitors would first call the studio, if no answer, they would then call four names on a list provided by the owner, **before they called the police.** I thought that was not good judgement. In the time it would take to dial four numbers the robber/employee could be gone. Make sure you know just what the procedures would be if the alarm sounds.

The other item concerns what happens if the phone lines are cut. As I understand the alarms, most work through the phone lines. If a perpetrator cuts the phone lines, there will be no signal going to the central station. However, if your alarm has been set up to sound at the location of the alarm, it will still sound even if the phone lines are cut.

There are two ways to circumvent that problem. Assuming there is underground telephone cable to the building or office, you can bring the telephone interface system indoors. This would probably not be possible in a leased space inside an office building. If the interface box is inside, the cable cannot be cut unless it is cut inside the office. By that time the alarm should have gone off.

The second way is to attach a cellular connection to the phone line. As I understand this, if the phone line is cut the line automatically flips over to the cellular line and the central station is called.

"Security cameras"

I think cameras are good if the exposure warrants the expense. The advantage of security cameras are once they and the video recorders are purchased and the cameras installed, there should be no more expense. The problem with most of the cameras that I have seen is that they are visible to anyone in the room. They can be vandalized and if the recorder is not secured, the tape or recorder can be taken. Cameras are good at watching over inventory, and in turn inventory control. If you have them where your working employees can see them, you will find that it will have an effect on the employees actions. It can also double as an eye witness to any events that take place within its watchful eye, such as interactions between employees, and work productivity.

"Security Guards"

Guards are better at keeping people out of the store or warehouse or parking lot area. In that regard, they would deter employee theft. But to prevent theft from within, other methods already discussed are more efficient and a lot less costly.

"Inventory Control devices"

This topic concerns wholesale and retail merchandise and inventory. You are probably aware of the "inventory tags" found on merchandise in retail stores. I am familiar with three types. The oldest is the beige colored two part piece that is found attached to clothing. If you walk through the doors of the store carrying an item with this tag, an alarm sounds. Sometimes someone will come, sometimes they won't. The second type of **"tag"** is newer and consists of an ink cartridge that is attached to the **tag**. If the **tag** is removed without the proper tool, the ink capsule is ruptured and the ink dyes the clothes so they cannot be worn without the obvious ink stain on it. The third type is a three dimensional inventory piece that is secured to the merchandise by glue, and must be neutralized by an anti magnetic type of tool in order for the customer to walk out of the store without setting off the alarms. I have seen these on stereo, and computer boxes. I have also been told they are available for smaller inventory such as liquor bottles. The problem is that once you de-magnetize the piece it is no longer usable, as opposed to the other two pieces that can be snapped back on to another coat or dress.

It is my understanding that all three items are placed on the inventory at the store or distribution center level. Their purpose is more to deter customer theft than employee theft.

Since most theft of inventory by employees, with the exception of collusion with a non-employee, is accomplished by taking the inventory out the back door or before the merchandise is brought into the store, you should rely on the controls discussed in the other chapters of this study or suggested by security people in your industry in order to minimize employee theft of merchandise and inventory.

Conclusion

It is my hope that by reading this book, you, the reader will have become more educated in the subject of employee dishonesty.

If everyone that reads this study can find just one item of new information or an idea for controls that will benefit either the reader directly, or who the reader shares the information with, then this book will have been a success.

Employee theft is big business, yet so many employers have no clue who steals, why, how, or what employees steal. It is this lack of exposure, experience and education of those that hire that provides the arena in which employee theft thrives. It is because of these three "E's" that the professional service advisor plays a very important role in stopping employee theft.

Any professional service advisor (insurance agent, accountant or attorney) has a duty to assist the client to the limits of the service provider's expertise, or at least provide the client his options regarding any professional services. You want to make sure the client receives complete insurance coverage, accurate and timely financial statements or sound legal advise depending on what your profession may be. Included in the services you offer should be information that is contained in this study. Failure to impart any of this information to the client may someday cause you to receive a distressing phone call from that client.

If **you are** the client (employer) please consider the information contained in this book. Discuss the important points with your professional advisors and company officials. Employees who are embezzlers are a lot smarter and cunning than most employers give them credit for. They can destroy your company if allowed to operate unchecked. Do not be deceived by an employee's years in service, personal and professional relationships, positions held, or the improbability that this employee would steal from you. If records do not match up, if cash is short when it should not be, if expense is higher with no obvious reason, you probably have a problem covered in this book. Remember this old saying, if it looks like a rat, and smells like a rat, it probably is a rat.

Always be alert.

R. W. Deckert

Appendix 1

SUGGESTED MINIMUM AMOUNTS OF HONESTY INSURANCE

Dishonesty Exposure Index		Amount of Honesty Insurance	
Up to ...... $ 25,000		$ 15,000............$ 25,000	
$ 25,000 125,000		25,000............ 50,000	
125,000 250,000		50,000............ 75,000	
250,000 500,000		75,000............ 100,000	
500,000 750,000		100,000............ 125,000	
750,000....... 1,000,000		125,000............ 150,000	
1,000,000 1,375,000		150,000............ 175,000	
1,375,000 1,750,000		175,000............ 200,000	
1,750,000 2,125,000		200,000............ 225,000	
2,125,000 2,500,000		225,000............ 250,000	
2,500,000 3,325,000		250,000............ 300,000	
3,325,000 4,175,000		300,000............ 350,000	
4,175,000 5,000,000		350,000............ 400,000	
5,000,000 6,075,000		400,000............ 450,000	
6,075,000 7,150,000		450,000............ 500,000	
7,150,000 9,275,000		500,000............ 600,000	
9,275,000 11,425,000		600,000............ 700,000	
11,425,000 15,000,000		700,000............ 800,000	
15,000,000 20,000,000		800,000............ 900,000	
20,000,000 25,000,000		900,000............ 1,000,000	
25,000,000 50,000,000		1,000,000............ 1,250,000	
50,000,000 87,500,000		1,250,000............ 1,500,000	
87,500,000 125,000,000		1,500,000............ 1,750,000	
125,000,000 187,500,000		1,750,000............ 2,000,000	
187,500,000 250,000,000		2,000,000............ 2,250,000	
250,000,000 333,325,000		2,250,000............ 2,500,000	
333,325,000 500,000,000		2,500,000............ 3,000,000	

SUGGESTED MINIMUM AMOUNT OF HONESTY INSURANCE

$_____

As indicated in the heading over the above table, the suggested amounts of Honesty Insurance shown are minimum amounts. They must not be interpreted as the maximum amounts which may be needed to fully cover any dishonesty losses that may occur and should be adjusted upward as deemed necessary in the light of your own individual exposure to such losses. Further increases should be considered in the amount of Honesty Insurance to be carried in recognition of the possibility of a catastrophic loss.

Appendix 2

1996 LAWS OF MARYLAND

CHAPTER 469

(House Bill 597)

AN ACT concerning

Employers – Disclosure of Information About Employee or Former Employee

FOR the purpose of establishing a presumption that certain employers who disclose information about the job performance of employees or former employees to prospective employers or under certain other circumstances are not liable under certain circumstances; granting to certain employers under certain circumstances a presumption of good faith which can be rebutted under certain circumstances; providing for the application of this Act; and generally relating to the disclosure of information about the job performance of employees or former employees.

BY adding to

Article – Courts and Judicial Proceedings

Section 5–399.7

Annotated Code of Maryland

(1995 Replacement Volume and 1995 Supplement)

SECTION 1. BE IT ENACTED BY THE GENERAL ASSEMBLY OF MARYLAND, That the Laws of Maryland read as follows:

Article – Courts and Judicial Proceedings

5–399.7.

(A) AN EMPLOYER ACTING IN GOOD FAITH MAY NOT BE HELD LIABLE FOR DISCLOSING ANY INFORMATION ABOUT THE JOB PERFORMANCE OR THE REASON FOR TERMINATION OF EMPLOYMENT OF AN EMPLOYEE OR FORMER EMPLOYEE OF THE EMPLOYER:

PARRIS N. GLENDENING, Governor   Ch. 470

(1)   TO A PROSPECTIVE EMPLOYER OF THE EMPLOYEE OR FORMER EMPLOYEE AT THE REQUEST OF THE PROSPECTIVE EMPLOYER, THE EMPLOYEE, OR FORMER EMPLOYEE; OR

(2)   IF REQUESTED OR REQUIRED BY A FEDERAL, STATE, OR INDUSTRY REGULATORY AUTHORITY OR IF THE INFORMATION IS DISCLOSED IN A REPORT, FILING, OR OTHER DOCUMENT REQUIRED BY LAW, RULE, ORDER, OR REGULATION OF THE REGULATORY AUTHORITY.

(B)   AN EMPLOYER WHO DISCLOSES INFORMATION UNDER SUBSECTION (A) OF THIS SECTION SHALL BE PRESUMED TO BE ACTING IN GOOD FAITH UNLESS IT IS SHOWN BY CLEAR AND CONVINCING EVIDENCE THAT THE EMPLOYER:

(1)   ACTED WITH ACTUAL MALICE TOWARD THE EMPLOYEE OR FORMER EMPLOYEE; OR

(2)   INTENTIONALLY OR RECKLESSLY DISCLOSED FALSE INFORMATION ABOUT THE EMPLOYEE OR FORMER EMPLOYEE.

SECTION 2. AND BE IT FURTHER ENACTED, That this Act shall be construed only prospectively and may not be applied or interpreted to have any effect on or application to any cause of action arising before the effective date of this Act.

SECTION 3. AND BE IT FURTHER ENACTED, That this Act shall take effect October 1, 1996.

Approved May 14, 1996.

Appendix 3

FIDELITY PROOF OF LOSS

_____ 19 _____

_____
(Name of Bonding Company)

_____ , hereby presents claim in the amount of $ _____
(Named Insured)

representing actual loss sustained as a result of default under Bond No. _____ , dated _____

Name of defaulting employee: _____ Soc. Sec. No. _____
Last known address: _____
Title of position held at time loss occurred: _____
Period of employment: From _____ to _____
Date loss first discovered: _____ By whom: _____
Date first loss reported to the Bonding Company or its agent: _____
Date(s) loss occurred: _____
Name of company carrying other applicable insurance: _____

DETAILED STATEMENT OF CLAIM
(Attach original vouchers)

Date	Items of Loss	Amount		Date	Credit	Amount	
					By Salary		
					By Cash Deposit		
					By Notes		
					By Commission		
					By Other Credits		
	TOTAL						
	LESS CREDITS						
	AMOUNT OF CLAIM				TOTAL		

It is expressly understood and agreed that the furnishing of this blank to the insured, or the preparation of proofs by any representative of the above bonding company, is not a waiver of any rights of the bonding company.

STATE OF _____)
) SS.:
COUNTY OF _____)

_____ , being duly sworn, deposes and says: that he is the _____

_____ of _____
                                                                                         (Named Insured)

the claimant herein, and that the statements above are true there being nothing suppressed, withheld or misrepresented by the claimant; that the amount of indemnity hereby claimed represents the actual loss sustained by the claimant and caused by the fraudulent and dishonest acts committed by the employee above named.

Sworn to before me this

_____ day of _____ 19 _____   _____
                                                                                                                       Insured

_____
                      Notary Public

PERSONAL AND COMMERCIAL INSURANCE
Any person who knowingly and with intent to defraud any insurance company or other person files an application for insurance or statement of claim containing any materially false information, or conceals for the purpose of misleading, information concerning any fact material thereto, commits a fraudulent insurance act, WHICH IS A CRIME, and shall also be subject to a CIVIL PENALTY not to exceed FIVE THOUSAND DOLLARS and the stated value of the claim for each such violation.

Appendix 4

SUBROGATION RECEIPT

CLAIM NO. _____

RECEIVED OF THE _____ INSURANCE CO.,

the sum of _____ Dollars ($ _____)

in full settlement of all claims and demands of the undersigned for loss and damage by _____

occurring on the _____ day of _____ A. D. 19___, to the property described in

Policy No. _____ issued through the _____ Agency of said Company.

In consideration of and to the extent of said payment the undersigned hereby subrogates said Insurance Company to all of the rights, claims and interest which the undersigned may have against any person or corporation liable for the loss mentioned above, and authorizes the said Insurance Company to sue, compromise or settle in the undersigned's name or otherwise all such claims and to execute and sign releases and acquittances and endorse checks or drafts given in settlement of such claims in the name of the undersigned, with the same force and effect as if the undersigned executed or endorsed them.

Warranted no settlement has been made by the undersigned with any person or corporation against whom a claim may lie, and no release has been given to anyone responsible for the loss, and that no such settlement will be made nor release given by the undersigned without the written consent of the said Insurance Company and the undersigned covenants and agrees to cooperate fully with said Insurance Company in the prosecution of such claims, and to procure and furnish all papers and documents necessary in such proceedings and to attend court and testify if the Insurance Company deems such to be necessary but it is understood the undersigned is to be saved harmless from costs in such proceedings.

In Witness Whereof _____ have _____ hereto set _____ hand _____ and seal _____ this _____

day of _____ 19 ___.

WITNESS:

_____

_____

By X _____ (L. S.)

BY X _____
OFFICER

(Notarization to be completed on losses where local law requires it.)

FOR INDIVIDUALS	FOR CORPORATIONS
STATE OF	STATE OF
COUNTY OF } SS:	COUNTY OF } SS:

ON THE _____ DAY OF _____, 19 ___

BEFORE ME CAME _____

TO ME KNOWN TO BE THE INDIVIDUAL DESCRIBED IN, AND WHO EXECUTED, THE FOREGOING INSTRUMENT, AND

ACKNOWLEDGED THAT _____ EXECUTED THE SAME.

ON THE _____ DAY OF _____, 19 ___

BEFORE ME CAME _____

TO ME KNOWN, WHO, BEING BY ME DULY SWORN, DID DEPOSE AND SAY THAT HE/SHE RESIDES IN _____

THAT HE/SHE IS THE _____ OF

_____ THE CORPORATION DESCRIBED IN, AND WHICH EXECUTED, THE FOREGOING INSTRUMENT; THAT HE/SHE KNOWS THE SEAL OF SAID CORPORATION; THAT THE SEAL AFFIXED TO SAID INSTRUMENT IS SUCH CORPORATE SEAL; THAT IT WAS SO AFFIXED BY ORDER OF THE BOARD OF DIRECTORS OF SAID CORPORATION; AND THAT HE/SHE SIGNED HIS/HER NAME THERETO BY LIKE ORDER.

_____ NOTARY

_____ NOTARY

81990